ULTRA MAGA MAN

At night and out of sight, the
California liberal transforms.

Arlo Bear

Grrrowling Books

CONTENTS

FOREWORD

He spends his days on the very lowest rung of higher education in Southern California. He can't be seen having any of these views during the day. But in the dark, when the panini crumbs are swept into the dustbin of history, a hero emerges. It is an unlikely hero. He didn't even feel the emergence of his powers until the world around him started burning and everyone was cheering. Still, he remained on the sideline. Then three things happened:

Elon Musk bought Twitter. A billionaire represents the common man more than elected officials in Washington. He could purchase the moon if he wanted to. Instead, he bought twitter. Boss move.

Will Smith slapped Chris Rock. I don't know why, but many people in Los Angeles took the side of Smith and it shorted a circuit on his logic board.

Biden talked about Ultra-MAGA Trump policies. You know, the ones that make America overly great again. The ones all of us should reject. People who REALLY want to Make America Great have no place in this republic. That was the message from a wisp of a shadow of a man who wasn't much to begin with. The candidate so many voted for in an unspoken contract with the mainstream media. They would promise not to call everyone "orange man" racist every night after "hollow man" won. It was a lie. A fragile lie that can be exposed if we just have the strength to stand up against it.

I transformed into Ultra MAGA Man. A hero for the people. A budding, mid-level administrator of common sense. A symbol of the ages. Even though I could never show my face in public.

Within the pages that follow, I address pressing modern topics which reflect the entrenchment of ideas. Enjoy the content chapter by chapter, or select a specific topic, or choose at random. There is no right way to read this book.

PROLOGUE

During the day, I'm just a mild-mannered, genderless human form gliding through the streets of Los Angeles. I go to work. I eat some kale. I try to look like I'm expressing a thoughtful choice each time I go to a public restroom. I pretend that homeless people are part of a street art exhibit designed to challenge the humanity of those around them to be better people - to serve them better. I identify aromatic shades of urine like a wine critic: salty, dusty with just a yeasty hint of hepatitis C? Don't tease, how close was I?

The collaboration between government entities and sidewalk living reform is working out so well that the performances are becoming SRO. It's one of the abundant gifts of tolerance and equity, just like the schools where my son currently majors in "getting through" with a minor in "doesn't know squat." But I know that the world - especially a world that includes California - needs something. It needs a hero.

So, at night, I become Ultra MAGA Man. I roam the thought pathways of modern America giving my opinion knowing that a simple doxing will probably result in losing my job and my friends. But someone needs to be brave in this time. Someone needs to come to the rescue before the San Andreas fault finally decides that it's not worth holding up all these morons, and it lets us slip into the sea.

I, Ultra MAGA Man, heed the call. In the following chapters, I will examine my daytime and nighttime personas. Will the ideas save lives? Certainly so. With no power comes no responsibility; however, this book will never aim to hurt anyone except the demented and powerful. If my aim is sometimes off, please understand that it's not easy being a superhero especially in these times. Still, I will lace up my cork boots like a pro. I will pull down the pillars of hypocrisy for those living under the oppressive structure that ruins our society.

The world is now ready for Ultra MAGA Man.

CHAPTER 1: EDUCATION

By Day

I love the fact that my children don't have any tests. Such a declaration in the staff room at my college, yields nods and words of agreement. What do tests do? They benefit the people who do well. They are discriminatory. Testing is not in the best interest of the underperforming masses. It also might offend the people who pledge their lives - well at least a good portion of the year unless there are meetings and then they get a half day with the kids and the rest of the day in training - anyway, it might offend the dedicated members of the teaching profession. After all, they are the front-line heroes of society. The daily Captain Americas.

Education

Sure, there are some worksheets that come home where the lesson seems to be predestined to agree with the teacher's viewpoints. What kind of teacher doesn't nibble around the edges of indoctrination? It's so much easier than establishing an expectation of excellence and then maintaining it over the years. It's so much easier to find satisfaction in shifting political views.

My son had to write about how evil guns were. I can't argue that unconditionally. Guns do kill people. I'm happy that my son's teachers can imprint that upon his psyche. It is a valuable lesson. You cannot un-shoot a gun. I see that and talk about that to others around me with clarity and purpose. I can't stop myself from looking at the list of sources for the paper and question how all of them can have the same overlapping series of points. Are there any important distinctions that need to be addressed when approaching this topic? Apparently not. Not in High School in California. Here, there is but one sentiment: guns are evil.

My 6th-grade daughter had her third half-day of the week.

There is a new way to grade and import those grades into the CMS that her school uses. Publicly, I find it charming that this kind of thing takes time out of the school day. I just need to find the time to dip out of my job, stabilize her in front of some streaming service and return to work. What kind of person doesn't have time to get their kid from school every day at 11:30 and take care of them? Not me. I value my time with my daughter and thank the school system for not providing teacher training outside of instructional time. It's a gift to me, the Californian dad. I am a better person. Fathers in other states must surely envy me.

It's best to get to the kids early. Pack elementary school with homework. Strain their attention span to its breaking point while they're still listening. Maybe get some social conditioning in there as well. Why shouldn't a drag queen be teaching literacy to your 3rd grader with story time, or, better still, stripping for your high-school student at a pride event? Read my lips. This is what progress looks like. Get used to it.

My oldest son was in virtual learning and graduated at the top of his class. He can't name any countries in Europe, but who really cares about Europe? He can talk about how few classes he had to take as a senior. He has a grade point average that is above 4.0. Wow. That must make him some kind of superhero. Maybe a modern Gen X superhero? Is there anything he can't do? We will never know. He didn't take any tests along the way.

By Night

Night comes and the rumbling begins. My brain scrambles. The transition begins, and I turn into Ultra MAGA Man. I begin to question the actions and elements of my daytime persona. Could society learn something from Ultra MAGA Man? Say it isn't true. Still, like all superheroes, I cannot hold back the transformation. It comes the moment I'm at rest and thinking clearly.

Of course, the kids need to be tested. What kind of system brags about graduation rates when they mean nothing? If the educational society keeps watering down what it means to be a high school graduate, eventually they will prioritize themselves out of a job. If the world sees no value in the outcome of high school, they will see no value in the educators that facilitate this level of education. The same people who complain about teaching to a test seem to be unable to teach to anything. I had a high school teacher tell me that he wouldn't levy any assessment that semester because he needed to make sure that all his testing materials were constructed with requisite psychometric properties of validity. He got that off a website article entitled "How to pass off your laziness as progressive." Making people prove that they've learned something is viewed as restrictive. Let me counter that by stating that teaching them nothing that they remember wastes the glorious tools of youth. They have neuroplasticity coming out of their - well - neurons. They need to soak things up while they are spongy.

Why is testing so important? Because there are correlations in education that can be traced back to levels of academic competency. A study, published by NCES in 2014, showed that 70 percent of those incarcerated couldn't read at a 4th grade level. Does that mean that every kid who reads at a 5th grade level is safe? No, but wouldn't it be great to clear out the jails by having the best education system in the world?

A warehousing model of high school keeps the society in a class static system. Nobody leaves the tier they are on. Everybody stays at the same level. I'm not saying that every year needs a test for every subject. I'm simply trying to advocate for the need for testing at some points along the process.

Social conditioning needs to stop. If you as a teacher want to raise a group of kids who have your values, then start reproducing. Don't look at the classroom as a means to subvert the culture of those in your temporary custody for the prime purpose of advancing educational goals. Too many educators have looked into elements of the greater worldview that hates Americans and decided not to combat or question this; they decided they should embrace it. Why not bring the flaws of a country and put them under the microscope so that the students can see?

Now, I am going to surprise you here and agree with some of what they do. Go ahead and shock our kids with the way people have behaved. Rock them to their foundations with the way we still do behave towards marginalized communities. Then pick up a map and take on the same issues in every other country. See if there is a timeline that puts America at the back of the list of those places trying to solve problems in all communities. There is some fundamental decency in the American civic culture that should also be put on display for kids to embrace, hold on to, and use as a guide. They are the ones who need to make the country better. Don't inject them with sickness after sickness and then complain about how they are not doing enough to promote a cure. That's not the way the human body or mind works.

Have teachers in the classrooms during school hours. Do not move them out unless there is a fire, earthquake, or tornado. A flood can be taught through in many circumstances. Issue waders to people on the first floor. The organization of instruction and the method of instruction can and should be agile and informed by the population, but the times should not. When a parent drops off their kid at 7AM and picks them up at 3PM, it is a contract. If the school breaks the contract, then students should be allowed to move to a school where they take it more seriously. Most jobs do not allow people to determine when they will be working. I know that some do especially nowadays in our post-Covid world. For most, however, this is a gift, so until all jobs are allowed this freedom, the schools must conform to the workday of the people in their districts.

Online learning needs to be for students who maintain a GPA of 3.0 and above. If a student can't budget their time and produce work that is above the standard of their grade, they need less freedom, not more. The option to take studies to the online platform (and this may change as the forum evolves) must be part of a reward system for those who can still accomplish the tasks of each class without experiencing the learning in the classroom. If you want to allow all students this option, there needs to be more training and preparedness from all involved parties.

One last third rail to touch before leaving education: Critical Race Theory (CRT). Ultra MAGA Man does not hate CRT. He just wants it treated like any other religion that is talked about in the classroom. Do schools present the Muslim faith as the one true faith in lessons to kids? Do they start talking about it in elementary room classrooms where some of the complex ideas might be simplified into dogma? No. Are public schools actively pressing their kids to accept Jesus as their Lord and savior? No.

CRT is a religion for a special group of believers. They may attract more members or fewer in the coming years, but don't push it into learning space with the idea of uniform acceptance. Let the message be part of an academic investigation that can be embraced or criticized in schools of higher education. Keep it out of my kids (and Mitt Romney's) binders until they know at least one country in Europe.

That's my honors student.

CHAPTER 2: TRANSPORTATION

By Day

I get up in the morning after a long night in the murky landscape of ideology. I brush my teeth. It's important to have good dental hygiene no matter what side of the aisle you are on. I get into my car and face:

Transportation

I drive to work. In California, that is a problem. It is a universal problem. I don't know anyone anywhere in this Golden State who does not have a transportation trauma used in similar ways to the C-word. Yes, Commute. I have solved some of the pressures by buying an EV. That's right. The Ultra MAGA views allow for clean fuels. We just don't have the same smug, self-satisfied look as we breeze silently through traffic. I park in a large, covered lot with multiple chargers. I plug in my vehicle while I work. There is a satisfying click as I pump energy from the grid into my personal mode of conveyance.

I'm not here to flash my liberal big city credentials, but if you insist on keep asking, I have two EVs. This puts me in the category of less than two percent of Americans. I drop this into my conversation in the staff room. It doesn't receive a warm welcome. People here don't like it when someone is more virtuous than them. It's accepted because people do like to have a friend who has two EVs and that is the price of knowledge. It will be a good story at a wine tasting or blood orgy, whatever these people around me do on the weekends. I've never seen one of them. They could be vampires for all I know. Actually, I've seen too many vampire movies and I can say that all vampires are young, beautiful, and erotically charged. This is the polar opposite of the staffroom at a California College. My crowd fits a different mode. We are old, neurotic, and certain we are going to die soon.

When I get done with my classes, I return to my vehicle. The full-time faculty have Teslas. I am not jealous. They deserve them. Sure, they didn't go back into the classroom after Covid, and I did. I shake that thought off. That's a MAGA thought, where performance and outcomes align into a system of rewards. How ridiculous. I like this holistic world in California where people get things without knowing how, and they keep them by saying the right thing to people in power. It's a great system for the people in power. I drive home bumper to bumper.

I check immediately to see if there are any high-speed pursuits. In LA, you get into your car, buckle up, check for high-speed chases, and then disengage the parking brake. Before you think I am exaggerating, there were in excess of 700 reported in LA my first year at UCLA. These events can add up to six hours onto my trip. How do I know this? Experience. None today. They should just do what they do in the Northwest. They passed a law in 2020 that makes it illegal for police to pursue a vehicle. HB 1054 will change all of that. Finally, people can be safe on the roads of a major metropolis. Of course, there will be growing pains. Recently, a kidnapper called 911 to tell them that the SPD was illegally pursuing him. He made some good points. Although the Seattle police broke the law and disabled his car with spike strips, he has a good case against them in civil court. That's the way to handle the situation. If every criminal receives damage awards, this country might just turn itself around. Now, back to the commute.

I pass a Big Blue Bus coming out of the UCLA parking structure. I used those when I was younger. I'd take them down to Santa Monica and walk along the promenade. Now, there's always a smell of fecal matter coming from the back seats. People who sleep there during the day don't always get the chance to dip off to unload their bowels. It's fine. It's good. It keeps them off the streets during working hours. That's a victory. It's like LA is a cake and if it looks good during the day, it's a hit. It's a party.

It doesn't matter that the people that the busses service are pushed to get a car to get to work. Cars aren't the problem as long as they are EVs, so it's like you're handing low-income people freedom by opening up the busses to become mobile shelters. It's the kind of out-of-the box thinking that keeps all the local governments solving the same problems year after year. The democrats will get voted out the moment they solve one. That's what they do to the republicans. The minute they solve issues, it's time to abandon principles and pull down the tide walls. Let the ocean swallow this place up again. And until then, give out bus passes at the methadone clinic.

There is a hill that comes down the grade from UCLA that is called Mulholland pass. I have passed it a thousand times in my life. I have never once been going over ten miles an hour during a workday. On the other side is the Valley. It's the place where hot and ugly have fused into a living hellscape called San Fernando. I'm able to use the HOV lane with my EV so, I breeze through this area. There is one train station in North Hollywood that connects the valley to the city. It has been predicted that even if you opened an In-and-Out burger place in the parking lot, it still would not be popular. People who ride this train are some of the bravest residents we have. They are duly rewarded by being dumped out at Grand Central Station or as I lovingly refer to it: the jewel of LA. This train does not go to any of the places where LA commuters go most. It does not connect to the airport. Why would it? That's not the point. The point is to have a train.

Which, inevitably, brings me to high-speed rail. As I near home, I look back to a vote that I made back in 2008. It was back before I realized my heroic Ultra MAGA nature. Or perhaps it is part of my origin story? I don't know. Anyway, I voted for high-speed rail. It was going to link California cities. I had lived in Japan for many years. I knew what a train system did for a society; I had seen it firsthand. A train system is a tool that extends into every neighborhood. It is a core element to the shared experience of that nation. Perhaps it was because I missed Japanese men in white gloves pushing me into a packed train car, but I voted for it. Since then, the budget has tripled, and the date of operation has been pushed back by six years, but it was still a good vote. And it will definitely get done. I'm certain of it. There is no way that this program could fail without ever carrying a passenger. I'm so confident in that, that I get into my car every day and go to work to help pay for it.

After only an hour and fifteen minutes, I have completed a 40-mile drive. Even the math is invigorating.

By Night

I lose sensitivity to emotional advocacy as the light fades. I drink a domestic beer, and something changes in me. It's like I'm connected to everyone who ever wore a trucker hat with fake mullet extensions. I don't fight the transition. There were nights when I did. We had company, or a Marvel Movie inadvertently made me aware of the greatness of people who have principles and power, or my kids played in a sporting endeavor where they made some important contribution. But tonight, there was no diversion. I could feel the power of Ultra MAGA flowing into my logical centers.

I know that expressing thoughts like this open me up to being called a Nazi. All critical thinkers in this age are subject to the claim. If asking questions about the most powerful societal centers of the time is indeed a trait of Nazi thought, I have grossly misunderstood the Nazi movement. I use my Ultra MAGA powers only for the good of mankind. Therefore, I reject the belief that any definition of adding accountability onto a system of ideo-aesthetic pleasure is the death of empathy. It extends empathy down the road to the people who work to make this country great. Again.

I own a Chevy Bolt. This car used to burst into flames before the battery upgrade. It could not be parked in a garage. It could not be depleted below thirty percent of battery power. It could not be charged beyond ninety percent of battery power. This slice of "driving safety" did not inspire confidence and it no longer got me to school and back on days when I taught at Santa Monica. I could always use my second car, but with gas clocking in at around 7 dollars a gallon on the West side, it felt a little like that final trickle of gas that goes into the tank was worth more than my health insurance. If a gallon of gas can pay for plastic surgery in Bolivia, then something is wrong. It's always big oil that gets called in front of congress to discuss their culpability in the huge problems their industry cause. Even Ultra MAGA man believes that they should be cleaned up and put under the microscope. I'll pay more money to see rainbows with spotted owls flying beneath.

When the policies of the left are short-sighted and lead to huge spikes in energy prices, I'd like to see some scrutiny of their tactics. When was the last time a group of pipeline protesters were called before congress to see if maybe their goals could be tempered with reasonable standards that might keep grandma warm during the winter? When was the last time any person who has GREEN stamped across his or her forehead has had to answer any question about the timeline for their goals? People simply nod along with these advocates like they are "anti-Nazis." Who would question an anti-Nazi? I certainly wouldn't. But what if their policies hurt people and make life harder for those who are decent people? Decent people don't always run to a microphone to project their philosophy forward. In fact, decent people are usually the ones who shy away from the power of the crowd. They are too busy doing things for their communities. Sometimes, they even drive diesel trucks, and they're still better than the Prius crowd who does nothing but drive twice as far to be seen by their peers twice as much.

The bus system should be scrapped in favor of self-driving vehicles that take people from one place and drop them off at another. One address to the next is the way forward. Dominos is delivering pizzas this way. It's time for the local governments to explore a system that serves the people who need to pick up their prescriptions at the drug store, but don't have the stamina to drag their walker a half mile from the bus stop. I know this seems like I'm solving a problem with something that might be expensive. This Ultra MAGA man is not beyond taking care of his fellow man. He is simply appalled by the idea that kids and grandparents are in proximity to viral meningitis and colostomy bags when they board a bus.

Trains have their place in society. Unfortunately, that society is the nineteenth century. That was the last time a train changed a life for the better in California. Pour resources into vehicles that pick up a passenger in one place and puts them in another place. It's what this generation wants. Convenience is a losing battle. Give it to them or they will stop working to fund your social security payments. That's not a threat, it's an iron-clad promise from a group of people who haven't settled on what the word truth means. It's a strong impulse. Question it at your peril. If you think that young people aren't working hard now, wait until they stop.

CHAPTER 3: ENTERTAINMENT

By Day

Wednesday is the most dangerous of the workdays. Everyone has shed the novelty of Monday and Tuesday. They can't quite grasp Friday. They are pissed off at the way the work week hems them in when their friends who work in the Industry sleep in late every day. It sparks envy. Woke envy looks for blood.

Entertainment

So, the conversation in the staff room turned to the new movies coming out that Friday. Perhaps in a self-conscious instinct to collapse the time between Wednesday and freedom, Janice brought up that her kids had drug her to the new Marvel movie last weekend. There was a low, but still audible expression of disgust in the room. It came from a couple of sources. There were the documentary people. This was the group who only allowed themselves to be entertained by real life. These people thought that fiction was frivolous and should be avoided at all costs. The fact that they taught English Literature never really found anything more than an abstract irony that was brushed away by the lack of value of all things done by modern society. The fact that they were the preacher from Footloose never occurred to them because they never saw the film.

The second group were basically lowing with the crowd. But they had a tint of guilty pleasure that asked Janice to continue with her story. Janice didn't need any encouragement. She was in the second stanza of her story before the Documentarians could hijack the story and turn it into a weekend watching restored cinema verité of the bourgeois in turn of the century Paris. The story that Janice watched was especially interesting because of a single plot point that she kept emphasizing.

There was a Latina introduced into Marvel. The first one. Numero Uno. The only part of the story that came close to that kind of engagement was the fact that her kids were able to see that the girl had two moms. Two affectionate, caring, indigenous moms. How was Marvel ever going to top that!

I almost made a joke. The fact that Marvel killed off both characters after only a minute screen time might show their commitment to the movement. They needed to do more for me to believe that they truly embraced marginalized communities. I resisted the impulse. It was Wednesday and I was a white man. On Monday, it might have gotten a rumble of approval and a slight smirk from Janice. On Wednesday, it is more likely to be dismissed with a sneer and some comment about how incremental justice was nothing to take lightly in the eyes of social advancement.

I never understood why they called a mass of flounder a school of fish. Until I worked at UCLA. An academic staff room is like a school of fish. Keep swimming with the group in the exact same direction and there is safety. One moment of lapse of concentration and the group leaves you behind. One flinch, expecting the group to behave a certain way, and the individual is left behind. It's not a sad story. It's a construction of precision and merciless consequence.

It was not like these people were humorless. I don't want to present them that way. There were days over happy hour appetizers that they would relax into a form that both entertained and allowed entertainment to cross the barriers of bitter intellect. They just had turned off many of their pleasure centers in search of justice. Their search for justice was so exhaustive that it didn't really matter if the outcome always favored those they elevated. Or more importantly, justice had to hurt those people they hated. That's what they wanted most. And it made humor hollow unless it served justice. The target of justice changed daily.

So, the pathways to humor got shut down. The routes to laughter were restricted and policed by others. Laughing was still in the room, but usually from pockets of trusted listeners. It did not get to the group until it was workshopped through gatekeepers. There was still room for surprise.

Janice ended her story with a heartfelt review of one part of the story. "Benedict Cumberbatch is an absolute dish." The group roared with laughter and Janice turned red. Everyone could agree on that fact. Janice curtsied like a princess and sat.

By Night

Let me be clear, there is no actual spandex or wandering looking for ways to MAGA up some part of my neighborhood. Spiderman would be sorely disappointed at what Ultra MAGA Man does on a given night. He is a tired superhero. He's put in a full day work and would probably rather binge something with a subtle message that life is worth the effort. Neither am I the soup kitchen liberal who fully commits to the betterment of the downtrodden. They are respectable people. They want to help.

Entertainment is an interesting window to the society. I want to see everyone thrive. I don't like the patterns that leave some people in misery. I want to find something that gets more of society into the gears of the mechanism that we call the United States. I want them to feel the warmth of saying the name of the country and lighting up with pride. I don't want to force this with a spotlight. I want it lit from within. This is a much harder goal. It was where entertainment used to align with my values. Unfortunately, it seems to be slipping away in many of the films I watch with my children. It doesn't make me angry or violent (as some slanted observers claim of Ultra MAGA Man); it makes me want to inspire people to appreciate what I see. It also makes me want humor to be open to any person brave enough to stand on a stage with a mic. I couldn't do that under penalty of the complete destruction of all full-sized trucks. I love full-sized trucks. Long beds. Flex tailgates. Towing capacity. Sorry, I love trucks.

First of all, true crime is the place where Ultra MAGA and woke converge. We both love to see crimes get solved. It's part of what gives me hope for humanity. A murderous rich person who accidentally pushed his wife into a woodchipper makes for great TV. We all agree, and we can all come together. Finding a shrine of murdered biographers on the property of a reclusive Bassoonist savant really makes for six hours of twists and turns that most woodwind performances couldn't come close to matching. We're good. We've converged for a moment. Congratulate circumstance, justice, and human suffering for bringing all of the impulses of both groups together. We can do this.

On to Marvel. OK. We're in trouble here. I didn't even know the girl was a Latinx. Don't blame me. Some people think I am Latino. I am pretty suave. I don't have the same radar for racial distinctions that Janice has. Maybe it's like tuning an instrument. You have to really concentrate and get every aspect of every string pulled to a very specific tension to get this stuff right. Anyway, we have a Latinx with two moms who she immediately kills. I don't know how I feel about that. If that happened in a right-wing film, it would be studied. What am I saying about right-wing entertainment? Can't even conceptualize how that would happen. That's healthy.

So, my concern is the concept that they are going to need to top the two moms' part. What does that mean? Are we going to see a character with three dads and a head of lettuce that represents mother earth? "Carry your earth mother with you, young Genderwalker, so that the climate will recognize your search for social justice and adapt accordingly." I see the value in putting people into situations where they are introduced to new characters and situations. But the mothers in this particular film barely speak. Are they both alcoholics in a grace period between abusive outbursts? Are they mother-earth good people who found an orphan and dedicated their lives to her? The playing field is somewhere in between those markers. Helping me understand the humanity of people who are also part of a group has value. Sneaking the group into the background does little to bridge the worlds. Imagine showing a little kid from Mumbai that there is an

Indian butler in one scene of the new Tom Holland movie. That's not the kind of image that signals progress. It just covers guilt.

Back to my joke. It's low-key hilarious that the first Latinx superhero has the power to - wait for it- cross borders. Didn't anyone bring that up in the meetings for inclusion? Maybe the next Asian superhero will carry around a graphing calculator. The next male, activist, liberal cis-gender white superhero can be Inner Conflict man. He is simply on a mission to get laid. We see you at the rallies dude. There is a zero percent chance you are that into cruelty free skim milk. You're not fooling anyone.

Not every film has to have a huge American Flag tucked around pure patriotic impulses to grab my interest. I am interested in a complex world. I'm just not as interested in the world that makes everything about my life into satire. You worked, went to school, raised a family, and bought a modest house in the suburbs. What a loser. He is not invited to our next gala. It's OK. My RSVP would have been returned with regrets anyway.

CHAPTER 4: GLOBAL WARMING

By Day

I am at the stage in life where I'm more of an observer than a conqueror. I realized this while walking on the beach with my oldest son. He is about to go off into the world. He looks at the wave headed for shore with a strategy. He is going to paddle out, catch that thing and ride it wherever it will take him. I'm interested in the power, the beauty, and the danger that it is to my house (even though it is several miles inland - it's a dad thing). As long as it stays in the ocean, I'm totally fine with passive appreciation.

My perspective has limits. It is not meant to be a net cast over an ocean. Nobody deserves to know everything. But finding some enjoyment in the understanding of a small part of the world that I call my own is the goal. Duality can be as good as any other guide to get me there.

Global Warming

Thursday was dry and hot. Not every Thursday is dry and hot in California, but it was February. Winter was over. The extended air conditioning season had begun. On a side note, paying 500 dollars a month to keep my house cool is a privilege. It's not a large house, and the bill makes me feel like it is. It makes me feel important. I would pay it even if my house were always at a static 92 degrees inside.

I walked down the hall to the teacher's room. It had ceiling to floor windows that afforded a great view of the pedestrians walking in Westwood village. It was a guilty pleasure to watch the homeless man at the Chevron station scare the tourists. His testicles always popped out when he stood. I didn't even understand the precise physics that made a man's testicles covered at rest, always surge forward when standing. It was breathtaking.

My appreciation of the consistency of what the man offered an unsuspecting world was interrupted by a concept raised by Jenny.

"The drought is actually good for the farmers."

I took the bait.

"How so?"

She went on to explain how sustainable farming had to be pressed into the industry. By force of the environment if necessary. They needed to learn that rivers belonged to the world, not them. The water table underneath them was drying up. They were in for a rude awakening soon.

She did not connect that awakening to the food chain that delivered her butter croissant, which flaked on the desk between bites. She was in the middle of making a class set of collaborative information gap exercises she had printed and copied thirty times.

I thought about pointing out her fetish of killing trees for the sake of something that would be in the trash ten minutes after her lesson, but it was still morning. Challenges are better for later in the day. I walked right into an argument by doing the one thing that people hate the most. I tried to solve the problem.

"Rainwater harvesting on a local level can save about 20,000 gallons of water a year."

She scoffed. "You think you can fix a drought?"

I knew the tone. I was in trouble. I had proposed that things could be done to make things better. Generally, that was not allowed. There were special circumstances where solutions were acceptable, but looking at Jenny, this was not one of them.

I thought I might get her on my side by triangulating. De-desalinization had shown some good progress over the years. The power could be provided by solar, and the ocean needed draining anyway (that last part was a joke that did not land). There were experimental water recovery systems that pulled moisture out of the air. It was like a sail that drained water from the baseline humidity. I tried to get her on my side by suggesting they all be placed in Florida. People in California education hate Florida. It's a tripwire to their inner rage. How could a populous coastal state not fall in line behind their lead? What was Florida thinking? It must be ignorance. Anything built outside of their own likeness was considered provincial: an unmannered, toothless version of stupid. She was finally tired of listening. My smug radar was not prepared.

"Sure, you can fix the drought." She pished a dismissal. Night started creeping in.

"But you can fix global warming?" Oh. I stepped on that cat's tail. Hackles and all. This was quickly becoming something I could not diffuse.

"So, you don't think that man-made global warming can be fixed?" For a moment time stood still. Woke priestesses waited in the shadows to be told over lunch how a breeder male had committed something akin to treason by suggesting that global warming might have processes beyond our control.

Do not back up the court reporter and notice that I had just been scolded for saying that droughts could be avoided by careful planning and clean new tech that might benefit the people who produce our food. That was ludicrous. The idea that we could change the global temperature, a scale billions of times more complex and interwoven with elements that ranged from the microscopic to the celestial, that was doubtlessly within our grasp. Jenny had it covered.

Luckily, I had a fail-safe conversation killer locked and loaded. It works in any staffroom in any college, but I urge novices that the degree of difficulty is high. Don't try this unless you can produce a level of smug conviction that is off the charts. Any sign of doubt is blood in the water.

"We aren't going to get anywhere with that until we reign in corporate greed and factory farming."

Sounding like you are a part of the orthodoxy is vital. But in some cases, the regular talking points won't put people at ease. They may question if independent thought has crept in through right-wing radio, or a Newsmax special. In these circumstances, you might have to create a crisis conjunction. Basically, make sure two random ideas collide in the framework of environmental rhetoric. They become worried that they've never heard the openly leftist positions used in tandem before. Are they out of touch? Did they miss some kind of MSNBC memo? During this confusion, you can make your exit.

Global warming is an existential crisis. OK. Is there a way to quantify the date that it will be irreparable? Is there a way to take this concern and turn it into individual action? I love people shouting with signs. It's my favorite recreational activity and I just can't get enough of it outside of every capitalist endeavor in the world. Power to the people.

I just like to see an individual seeking to institute these ideas into their daily routine. That's convincing. All of the teachers who gave up their cars the day they converted to rigid global warming advocates are the heroes. I mean, I love to hear them talk about the virtue they want to impose on other entities. It's great. It's aspirational and beautiful.

I just want to ask if their hamburger came from a special cow that eats methane and burps potassium hydroxide. Their behavior rarely comes up. And that's actually good.

We need more windmills. Cervantes had it right. If they're not there. Create them. They will save you and fill you with righteous fury at a world that cannot see what you do.

There is no downside to solar. It's the sun. People have been worshiping it for millennia. Get on board and put it everywhere. I want to have a solar toothbrush that requires me to be outside to use it. Think of all the water that would be saved.

America can lead the way and other countries will follow. It's always been that way. We teach the world how to behave. We are the social equivalent of a non-invading colonizer of thought. People fall in line when you are right. Just look at all of the right things you've said in the staffroom. None of them have been challenged in the least. It is in this cauldron of the least skeptical listeners in the world that the best ideas come from.

By Night

My car produces a fake whirr that announces quietly that it is there. It's just loud enough to be annoying. And just quiet enough to be useless. It is the American left in a nutshell.

Why is fixing a problem considered the last stage of political thought? Why can't the solution be the first thing that people embrace? I know that solutions are messy, and problems are much easier to identify than fix; however, it would be just peachy if people who look for ways to solve issues might not get collectively shit upon. I think finding water for a farmer is actually more important than removing the carbon produced by three busses from the air. We have already discussed this; nobody is in those busses anyway. You can't cancel the route! That would be cruel. Where would the homeless go to the bathroom? I'm drifting. I apologize.

The complaints of a young, active political class should be heard. I just don't think they should drown out the machinery of the fix. Awareness has replaced personal responsibility and that is a lot of carbon coming out of mouths instead of sweat coming off of the skin. We could use the water.

Prove the existential nature. The first Earth Day in 1970 predicted the earth would not exist in thirty years. There were claims that mass starvation was unavoidable in the next ten years. These were noted environmentalists. I mean. Meteorologists have the same batting average. A person with a PhD doesn't control the tides. Find a way to use data over the past to convincingly shape a timeline. Make it one that both sides of the debate have issues with. It should represent skeptical thought and rational conclusions. Then, decide if you want to invade India and China to achieve climate goals. These are the most populous places on the globe. They are also large contributors to the greenhouse effect. Make the presentation worthy of an ultimatum. This ultimatum will be backed with a military draft of all of those who consider this problem worthy of war. The left wing of America will be the hawk that saves the planet. It will be brutal, but that's what existential threats require. Birkenstocks might be the new army boot. I really worry how they'll handle the jungles of Hainan.

Ultra MAGA man might surprise you on the burger thing. I like the plant burgers. They are tasty and if only inflation can make everything so expensive that they don't seem like much of a luxury, I'll buy them in mass. I also visited rural England and met some cows. They are such sweet things. I do not have a problem with ranching or raising beef or dairy cows. I just seek solutions that might limit the need to put any more animals than necessary into the food chain. Except for chickens. Those things deserve it. They are tasty and I just don't feel attached. Superheroes have complicated backstories. Maybe a chicken attacked me just before I fell into that vat of critical thinking books.

Windmills are great. They aren't super ugly. Ok. I am a little concerned that environmentalists who say that offshore oil rigs are a blight on the landscape are fine with white seizure-inducing perpetual motion machines are the answer to our power problem. Every twenty years, those things need to be replaced. Is that sustainable? We need a little more data before I jump on one of the blades and treat it like a ride at Disneyland. I'm willing to be convinced, but I'm also concerned that people jump to a conclusion and then build up reasons after it's part of their core beliefs. It is a flawed system for all of those except the brilliant. I'm worried at how many liberals think that they're brilliant these days.

Solar makes me hopeful. Right now, it's the equivalent of the tip on a meal (with a very cheap customer). It's not what sustains the grid. Can that change? Are the toxic chemicals that part of the solar panel landfills an issue? I am not a chemist, but some of the chemicals sound scary. I mean Erin Brockovich scary. Cancer cluster scary. Do I expect this to be the case? Not really, but I also didn't see Covid coming. I'd rather be very protective of my local environment while saving the planet.

The idea that American can lead the world it preventing global warming is a remnant that leftists killed. We are not the shining example of virtue. We've been told that by textbooks, talking heads and politicians certain that making American great is the problem. You've just popped the balloon and you're blowing into the intake lip even though the entire neck is blown. It will not inflate. It cannot fly. Why would the world like to be led by a group of people who are so flawed that half of them are Nazi, racist, narcissistic anime fans? The world will follow in line if we prove ourselves as the greatest nation on earth. They don't want to be led by flawed losers. Start talking up the American dream as a concept that has a future as well as a past and watch the temperature come down. Everywhere.

CHAPTER 5: TAXES

It's Friday. I don't think I have the kind of money in the bank that will allow me to go out to lunch. All of the full-time faculty go out to lunch. They bring back their bags from Baha Fresh and the latest combo salad juice bar across the street (there have been three). Nobody in the room talks about money. It's kind of embarrassing that the people who are on salary do the exact same work as the rest of us for twice the pay and half the accountability. Math was never my thing, but that doesn't sound fair. The room usually broods over fairness when it is in another state, or another country. When it is in their backyard, they look at the other people on their level and complain about what they don't have.

Money is not the center of my life. I can't put such an unknown on that axis. It's not always a sign of great character, intelligence, or ethic. I keep telling myself that at least. Maybe I'm too busy ignoring the people below me in the equation to get a good idea of the total picture. That does seem to be the trend.

Anyway, I tell my kids that wealth is not the goal. Character creates a broad path forward into life. It gives room for experimentation and conformity alike. People who put money at the center of their lives have a balance beam width way to progress. One slip and the money is gone, and there's really nothing left to pick up. The core of many rich people is a hollow confusion of pliant principles. Be sorry for them next time they look down on you. Or just curse their existence and get on with your day. That's my go to move.

My son has a hard time buying the "poor is noble" concept. On this particular morning I decide to describe it a different way. Being poor breeds a thousand kinds of suffering. Having money only achieves one thing of merit. It allows a person to create his environment. It gives that person the ability to make decisions about his or her life like he is the artist, and the world is their canvas. Nothing they think of cannot be produced. In the corner, there can be an elephant. Or more likely a tennis court in the backyard (that is soon turned into a pickleball court when they decide that running is something that only the last generation of rich people did).

The secret tragedy is that most of these people are not artists. They create stick figures around themselves. Pits of abundance that generate anger at the way they don't please enough. Instead of frantic creation of new worlds of joy and prosperity, they often sink along with their decency.

Taxes

The commute is dictated by a concept that Californians call "Friday Light." It has no meaning. I get into the office five minutes late. The copy machine is busy. This is a tragedy to any teacher who is pushing the boundaries of preparation. I can wing it. I have the book. Do I have the book? I can borrow a desk copy of the book and make copies when I start an active learning exercise.

Panic. Was I supposed to be at a meeting on sustainability? Ben notices my anxiety and calls me over.

"Yo." He used to be a drummer in a band. He still gives lessons on the side. That makes him about fifteen times cooler than anyone in the room. Including me. Twenty in my case. "I saved you a bagel from the sustainability meeting."

I ask him if he signed me in. He did. We get fifteen dollars for every meeting we attend on our own time. Our time. If that sounds confusing, it's just a way to show outreach to the part-timers. Wrapped in minimum wage rewards.

"Do we get paid today or Monday?" He asked.

This is the lifestyle of most of the middle-class Californians I know. Can we get our check before the first of the month so that we don't have to wait to pay down our credit cards far enough to extend our indulgent struggle out another month? It's not pathetic. I need to make sure I make the point twice, nothing pathetic about it. It's fine. It's dignified actually.

The nation and the state that I love and hate took almost 40 percent of the money I "earned" last month.

Taxes will not go up on the middle-class. That's the mantra of each political entity since the formation of wealth started when George Washington opened a better grist mill for his neighbor's crops. Nobody is coming for the paycheck of the middle class. I agree. I find it charming that the money I make and the money I take home are such a different amount. It makes sense.

I get so much for the taxes I pay. I comment on this as I chew my charity bagel and plan to spend my stolen fifteen dollars. The entire coast should have a halo over it. And an umbrella. It's so drenched with efficient government schemes that make the lives of its inhabitants better. I get the excitement and adventure of driving on roads that may or may not be pitted with holes. I get street entertainment including testicle surprises that are so Avant Garde that I can see an award coming soon for Man Standing, the one-man show of Westwood.

I feel like the taxes are being spent wisely. The money I spend myself seems so selfish and disconnected from greater societal goals. I really appreciate the focus that government brings to the process. They know how to make decisions that prioritize the prosperity, health, and happiness of the population they govern. It's inspiring.

By Night

My wife tells me these transitions are getting tedious. Since she is the smartest person, I know. I will take her advice. From this point forward, I will only make the shortest introductions referencing my transition to Ultra MAGA Man. Or maybe I'll just keep doing it to frustrate her. Ultra MAGA Man does have a sense of humor after all.

To take money from citizens in order to ensure efficient governance is a valid and even virtuous endeavor. I just don't see why the government wants a loan-shark levels from the people who go in to work every day. The usury rates are capped at ten percent in California. That means they tell people in the lending industry that ten percent is the most you can charge; anything more would be punitory. The tax rate is 13 percent. Is punishment something else when it is done by elected officials? I think I'm missing something. It's usually money, that is deducted before I see the bottom line.

Does anyone believe the claim that both parties make about never taxing the middle class? How did the rate get to where it is without collusion among the parties? They both show complete disdain for people who work to pay their salaries. They want attention. They are moths to the twitter flame, and they have an attention span that can't be considered healthy. The next time I hear that the middle-class won't be paying, I want everyone in America to shout at the screen with the same anger and disgust that they have for European sports (I'm looking at you badminton) or the egos of social influencers. "NOOOOOOOOO!" It may get the attention of someone passing and frighten them into delaying their plans on bankrupting the nation for a few more years. That's really the best outcome the middle-class can ask for. Solutions are not on the table. Just an extension of ineptitude and waste. It's not a great bargain but hold your nose.

How can anyone look at the quality-of-life decline and think that taxes are being spent wisely? The government used to pick up my trash when I was young. They used to put criminals behind bars. They used to build roads and keep them at a level that was never termed as automotive reckless endangerment. Everything that requires active solutions have been privatized. The world has looked at central control and rejected it when it touches any part of their lives. If liberals see anything working, they try to defund it or give it to their uncle's company as a contract in public-private partnership. I will take the military and justice systems out of this equation. I believe they are doing their best. They are neither respected or admired the way they should be for standing up and demanding some kind of standards of behavior in the country and the world. Beyond, that find one institution that is not under attack when they do their jobs well, and I'll argue that it's the first.

I send three kids to public schools. They are well-meaning centers of inefficient design. That's the end of the list of things (above the level of basic competency) I get back from my local government. I mean, the streets are relatively clean and safe because I'm in a wealthy suburb that aligns more with conservative values on these points. So, there is a basic level of services that does get done. But am I wrong to expect more? Why can't we have schools that are looked at as the top in the state? There were smash and grab robberies at the mall down the street. Nobody was prosecuted. People were caught and allowed to give back the merchandise. Are we so addled that this is justice? My grandfather would have made me pay back the company for the broken glass. He would have made me apologize to the owner. Nobody will ever have as much honor as my grandfather did. He was a war hero and paraplegic giant. I just think that when his standards as a citizen are not met by the justice system, it no longer really holds the necessary respect.

California spends 7.2 billion dollars on homeless issues. They spend less than a billion on parks and recreation. How many people reading this has gone through a park? How many has taken their kids to a soccer game? What did this mean to the lives of the children and adult population that spend their time racing through office work to get home for the weekend and find some enjoyment? Well, the government values this at 1/7 of the value of programs that have done NOTHING to reduce a homeless population. If a program doesn't show consistent results, it should be cut. Every audit should come out with an efficiency sheet that is produced based on the goals the program sets out for itself when it gets the money. There should be a mandatory cut off of all government funds if the metric falls below a certain level of efficiency. If people are paid to get results, they might. If they are paid to extend the issue into infinity, that sounds like a better retirement plan. I'm not commenting on lazy workers. I'm attacking the corrupt contracts that push promises forward and bury results. These people have roamed the middle-management of government for too long. They have become complacent and purposeless. Give them something new to do. Maybe they can don a suit and join the Ultra-Mega Maniacs?

CHAPTER 6: THE POLICE

By Day

Saturday is a day of fun. It's not the time to confront core problems in a society. So, in line with that, I've chosen to take on a topic that has not been at the disastrous tectonic chasm representing the divide between the politics and society. It is the only job where matters of life and death are public record. If a doctor ever had to worry about people protesting his residence because of a slip of the scalpel, we'd all be headed to Canada for medical treatments. I would still never go to Canada. They don't treat their truckers right.

The Police

This topic is not aided by the depiction of police in films of my youth. The sheriff was always presented as the center of virtue, power, and righteous retribution in the American Western. We grew up idolizing the badge in a way that could not possibly be in line with a profession that numbers tip the scales at nearly a million. If all the police officers in America moved to Wyoming (a beautiful state) it would double the population. Not only that, but the convenience stores in Wyoming would NEVER have a problem with crime. Literally. They could leave the cash register pointed towards the customers and never see a dollar taken. Just too much exposure if every other person is a cop.

So, there is an impossible standard for being in law enforcement. That doesn't mean that the profession doesn't deserve scrutiny. It is one of the most popular topics of conversation in the staff room. It's easy. There is absolutely no dissent. Everyone believes that cops are racist, trigger-happy alpha males. The only thing up for grabs is which of the descriptors is most damning. The room usually agrees that the alpha male part is the worst depending on the day.

I have to admit here that I have had a bad experience with a policeman myself. I was 19, driving seven miles an hour over the speed limit in rural Montana when I was pulled over. I was visiting my Grandmother in Billings (a woman whose kindness tipped the scales at an unmeasurable increment), and I was going to be getting in just in time for breakfast. It was 3AM and the sheriff who clocked my unforgivable transgression against regional speed laws put me through the paces. I gave him all of my documents. He asked where I was going at 3AM. I told him I was going to visit my grandmother in Billings. He scoffed. What kind of person visited his grandmother at 3AM? I noted that I was four hours away from Billings, and she was an early riser. Not really the worst thing a Grandson could do was to surprise her on the way home from college.

He then asked me to pay the fine in cash on the spot.

I summoned up my courage and said no. OK that's a lie. I didn't have any money on me, or I totally would have caved into an authority figure demanding anything while shining a flashlight in my eyes.

He didn't believe me. Everybody caries cash on the road.

It was probably true. Cash was everywhere in my youth. Nobody left the house without cash. It was a different world. No Venmo. No Apple Pay. I just was at a moment in my life when money was scarce. I was on financial aid at my school. I had two jobs, but they were intermittent because of my school schedule. I had a bank card and a checkbook.

This did not impress the officer. He demanded payment or he would have to take me to jail for the night.

I don't know if I called his bluff or simply had no other options. I told him that he'd have to take me to jail. I asked if they were going to tow my car or if I could drive it to the jail behind him. My commitment to the role of incarcerated teen (I was a theater major at the time) must have tripped something in his logic centers. He agreed to take a check.

He warned me through the window that if it did not cash, he'd look up my grandmother in Billings and show up on her doorstep. It was kind of a mixed bag in the repercussion department. I had not given him the correct address. Granny was safe. But the check did cash. I should leave that part out, but I'm still worried that the cops' offspring from Beaverhead County might surge forward and try to collect the dept.

Teachers are the most sheltered people in the world. Teachers at UCLA have thirty more layers of protection between them and reality than those in the standard population. Yet they seem to have opinions that burst the bubble of their existence. They have ideas about how to do two jobs in the world. Their own. And the police.

The police have a history of racism that cannot be denied.

This is a proclamation in a room where everyone is white. There is one Iranian woman in the corner, but she is not participating.

Everyone agrees. It's like the short story "The Most Dangerous Game" and all people of color are under the unrelenting pursuit of General Zaroff.

The profession just draws the wrong people. They don't have degrees. They aren't like everyone in the room. It is a point.

The discussion ten years ago was that all the department needed was leadership from marginalized communities. More Latino and black leaders would make the police more accountable. Then, they saw that law enforcement people of all color wanted to enforce the law. So, they cooled on that idea. It must be the idea of justice that is truly racist. How could anyone agree with so many people of color in jail? Numbers don't lie.

The statement is pretty rich, because if I were to bring up a number they didn't like (like only six unarmed black men were killed last year by law enforcement) they would shout me down the corridor as a confederate sympathizer, brown coat, Kristallnacht reenactment enthusiast.

It's not just racism, the entire model of policing seeks to oppress. There are people out there stealing baby formula (don't get me started) and bread. The institution of law enforcement wants them all on death row. The police will allow people like Madoff to steal for years, but one 7-Eleven clerk gets a Saturday night special shoved in his face, they freak out. And do they get proper representation after their cash bail? That's another topic.

Police don't act like human beings in their interaction with the public. There was one guy who gave one of the teachers in the room three jay-walking tickets over the past year. Put the absurdity of recidivist j-walking in the back of your mind and she implores the room to understand her point. He was smug and condescending each time. He didn't acknowledge her as a human being. I have a little sympathy for this particular criticism. Even though the job is clearly stressful, it should be part of the training to portray the badge as humble, generous, and kind- even if it is unwavering. I had a cop pull me over for being in the HOV lane. I had a crying toddler in a baby seat in the back. When I asked if the kid counted, he didn't even crack a smile. He asked for my paperwork and mumbled something about how the stop was my fault even though I'd established that it had no cause. My child cried as he looked for something else to charge me with on the side of the road. In the end, he handed everything back and said in a stern tone that I should not enter traffic until the next break. If that is a model of human interaction, we are in trouble on levels that have nothing to do with law enforcement. There are elements of decency walk alongside every job being performed in this country. Everyone is wise to correct course if they find that element of themselves diverting from them during work hours.

Police take resources away from the real heroes of the city: the social service professionals that should be deployed instead of officers. Yes, that sounds right. Send in a civilian to deal with a violent outburst in a home. They will certainly have the authority to deescalate the situation. It sounds good when you're in the staffroom, but I'm not sure how serious these alternatives are taken. I would not be very relieved to find a social service representative respond to my report of a group of kids stealing catalytic converters outside my home. She might be able to talk them down, give them the resources to speak up and find a better, more productive place in society, but they might just laugh and run away. This never occurs to the room. Any way, if the social services people can't handle it, there's a number for the department of behavioral health if the situation really gets out of hand.

By Night

I'm having drinks with friends when my veil drops. I mention that my SWAT trained neighbor makes me feel a little better about living on the street. It's a test balloon. It is welcomed quietly. People who live in the suburbs can sometimes talk about safety as if it is a priority. If it's in small clusters. And nobody is around.

The police are not racist. The law is not racist. It is a set of rules that delineate unfavorably along the line of rich and poor. The sins of the rich get overlooked. The sins of the politically favorable get overlooked. Everyone else just has to navigate the world. It is not an easy task. People who have one misstep should be given all of the benefits of society to get them back into the world and on track to their individual greatness. I don't know how many of the people I admire most have been arrested at least once, but I'd imagine that it's a higher number than I'd guess. Breaking the law is presented as the solution when there is no opportunity presented to the people. Keep presenting the opportunities to the poor and keep putting the people in jail who hurt those who are trying to pursue a pathway that makes this country great. People who hate America are not all criminals, but I sometimes see laws aligning to protect that hatred. It's just another kind of bigotry. Police have a thin line to tread in a constantly changing environment. They have sins themselves. Treat them the way you would an activist who promotes your favorite policies. Back them until it crosses a line. Urge everyone to make the lines easy to see and impossible to cross.

The police don't arrest rich people. Well, the entire society bends rules around the rich. How many nephews have jobs that they don't deserve? Do they deserve their position? No. Do they have it? Yes. How does a restaurant treat a rich patron? How does a school treat a rich benefactor? How does the medical profession treat a person who donates the money for a new wing of a hospital? They become saints. Sure, their money comes from indescribable suffering, but it's clean when it pours into the small inlet of society that you care about. That doesn't mean that we give up on parity and equality under the law. Just point the spotlight in all of the directions the idealism finds targets. And don't be surprised when it illuminates something you like. It's part of the disinfectant part of governance. Keep at it until all professions have expectations of both tolerance and accountability. Buy the cop a cup of coffee as you crusade. He might be nicer to the next perp.

The collective cop personality is a bit of an unfair judgement. If you looked at the personalities of the teachers I'm around, you'd find a range of back-stabbing power-thirsty, manic control freaks, to honest, intellectual inspiring role models. That's in one room at a decent University. Character is a rabbit hole. If you go down it, be ready to look at the character that surrounds all human endeavors. I say this not because I want to shift focus away from bad Cop behavior, but because I think that if we are being honest, character is in short supply in every profession in the modern world. I want to look up to the police, so I am willing to MAGA the training and review of the people in whose hands we trust our safety and welfare. Maybe seek to put more officers in contact with the people they protect. I know that the mounted policeman who gave me finger guns when I was a kid watching a parade in old town Arvada Colorado made a big impression. I saw him later put a toddler up in the saddle with him. Maybe it's the fact I was brought up in the old west, but I want my policeman to be the person who sets everything right in the world and then deflects the praise of a grateful community with a nod and a smile.

"It's all part of the job."

CHAPTER 7: SPORTS

I've made it to Sunday. There is no better day on the calendar for families. I don't have to listen to the mealy drone of daily commentary from people who can't pry loose a single shred of humanity for those who stand right in front of them. They are much more excited about people who kneel or swim in contests far away and yet somehow vital to their own concept of identity.

Sports

"Kaepernick and Lia Thomas really got it right." This was my boss in a curriculum meeting before sharing her minutes from the last meeting on how to dilute the expectations of the core classes so that they might end up as meaningless as delineation between gender. No. Nothing could be that meaningless. I mean how could the ancient concept of male and female - reinforced through every creature ever produced in a zygote system of genetic collaboration between two parent organisms - how could that have any standard meaning in society? Who came up with that bigoted system? It was probably a man. Or was it?

Kaepernick is a championship-caliber quarterback who simply raised a small point about how racist white society is in America and found himself blackballed by the song police. That's what the people in the English Department believe. To the core. Most have never watched an entire football game. This does not mean they will not go to the mat for a poor kid trying to call out a system for the suffering of his people. It makes sense. This guy was the best quarterback in the league. He went to the Superbowl and I'm almost certain he won and set records for his position that will never be surpassed. He was a one-man wrecking ball of intellect, ability, and timing. Sure, there's video tape of a running back who knocked out his girlfriend with a sucker punch in an elevator. That guy received a two-game suspension. The most brutal black eye to the NFL in recent memory and the guy was out for a grueling two weeks. It certainly didn't have anything to do with the fact that he was a key offensive weapon who was coveted for what he did on the field. That doesn't fit the Kaepernick narrative. If you're amazingly great in the NFL, you get a one-way ticket to Palookaville just for taking a knee. This punishment was replicated throughout the sports world. I remember. Every member of every team who knelt while the Star-Spangled Banner was being played (totally overrated song by the way - why do we even play it) was punished in the same way. I feel for those volleyball players from Delaware who knelt before their game. I mean, all of their lives ruined? It just isn't fair.

Talking about fair, this next one is going to be trouble. The discussion of any elements of gender ideology leads often to the claim that the speaker is indecent and ignorant. Granted. We are all on a path forward trying to correct the elements of our character that are not up to the challenge of almost daily change on a range of issues. But now we must investigate the possible indecencies of the other side. See if they can own up to the arguments that they never hear in this one-sided presentation of validation and rights.

Anyway, Lia Thomas is a perfect role model. Gandhi just freed a nation. Lia freed every swimmer who ever decided to change their gender with an eye for the prize. Condemning this act is ignorant. It's the identity equivalent of subjugation. This was a man who decided to change his gender. Who are we to challenge this? By the way, Ultra MAGA man doesn't even care about this part that much. Personal choice is a central part of the great American experiment. If you want to move to Yuma and plant turnips, you can do it. You want to marry your dog, please don't consummate. You want to claim gender is your personal playground, fine, just don't start demanding treatment that is reserved for more traditional female females.

Lia won a race by 38 seconds. Against athletes who had trained their entire lives in the sport. That just tells me that the other girls are lazy. They didn't do enough to beat Lia. It's really just an ugly attack to bring up anything about the differences between men and women at all. In women's sports it's particularly galling. What are you doing for the young trans athlete who wants to become the top of women's sport or for those transitioning the other way clinging to the bottom rungs of male sports? She is a trailblazer and the haters come out in force when they see a target so authentic, so steeped in dignity. There's just no other explanation for it.

By Night

I am at a microbrew bar with my wife. We are watching sports, but it's not a sports bar. In California, we have craft bars with multiple sporting events on TVs surrounding the tavern-style environment. It's just a place where people pay 9 dollars a glass for a beer that has accents of honey and suckle. It's away from the kids. And during a commercial break we get to talking. My wife used to be a socialist with Maoist tendencies. She has shifted since seeing the deductions in her paycheck that go to feed das Kapital.

"Was Kaepernick any good?" She asks me with sincerity. I can feel the transition coming on. I want to down another Willma's Lingonberry and vanilla ale and just gulp down my own opinion on the subject. But it rises in me. I transform. My Ultra MAGA ideas spill out before I can even articulate a proper trigger warning to the neighboring tables.

I explain that he was competent. He had an awkward delivery. He had tools, but his results were up and down. Too many of the plays were down. He seemed to be the kind of QB who the league caught up with and he met the challenge with limited enthusiasm to respond on his own part. It was easier to be a social Icon than a great QB. The very act of kneeling might sum up his contribution to the sport. When the toughest challenge of his career came, he looked for reasons to lash out against how unfair things were. It's more of a commentary on his maturity than anything else. He could have been great. Most of that challenge was on his shoulders. Was he going to stand and deliver? Or kneel and complain? We know the result. It's just the explanation that hangs over the sport. Was it racism? Ask yourself as a football fan if Patrick Mahomes could burn down the capitol and get a fully guaranteed contract with the Browns. If you answer yes, because it is a sport where unique merit triumphs over almost any defect of character, I'd agree.

Lia Thomas is a role model. Well, I have to dance around that one. Living an authentic life is a triumph. Does that include the privilege of taking part in sporting competitions whose guidelines were meant to preserve the achievements of biological women? Ultra MAGA Man might surprise readers here. I am all for her competing with women or men or anyone she wants to. It just belongs outside of the realm of collegiate or professional sports. Achievement there is reserved for women who were born with advantages in all aspects of life except body strength. Taking this space away from women is selfish. Compete on the local or club level until you're satisfied that your competitive spirit has been sated. It's a great hobby. Changing gender turns sports into hobbies. It's not cruel. It's not personal. It pays respect to the gender you have so much inner overlap with. It's in fact the only just way to allow female achievement to be acknowledged.

Is this position earned? Is it thoughtful? Well, whenever an athlete wins a swimming race by 38 seconds, some soul searching needs to be done. Secretariat beat Twice-a-Prince at the Bellmont. He did it by the largest margin ever achieved on the course. He was 31 lengths ahead. That converts to about six seconds ahead of the next horse over a mile. So, six seconds in horse racing was a mockery of every contest that ever came before that day in 1973. Now, a lot has happened since the 70's. I'm first to admit this. But dominance is something the eye cannot deny. When we see a contest that isn't really a contest, it gets awkward. This leads me to my last point.

Where is the damn shame? Why does a biological boy look for attention beating women? It seems so embarrassing and toxic. Where are the people saying - sure, you can do it, but why would you - that's the crowd I'm inviting to my next Ultra MAGA event. Competition can also be dangerous. An MMA transgender fighter who later married and had a kid with his girlfriend, gave his female opponent a concussion and broke the orbital bone that protects a person's eye socket. She is now an icon. What an ugly badge of honor to carry around. It's pathetic. Beating up a woman with the strength of a man is the kind of deficiency I cannot dive into and come out unchanged on the other side. Instead, I brand it sickness and keep it at a distance. This is the worst of the examples. There are transgender skateboarders losing money and endorsements to people in male bodies. I just find that to be unfair and destructive to women. I can still be convinced going forward that it's not just a grab by men who seek glory and attention at all costs. As soon as a transgender woman to male wins in an individual competition, I'll be closer to being convinced about the equality of modern gender building products. At that point, maybe we've found the chemical balance that favors fairness over stubborn biology. That day will probably come, but until then, no money, no glory for people who take the podium away from biological women.

CHAPTER 8: ABORTION

By Day

OK. I am into standing up for women. I grew up in the West. We take pride in being there when needed by our sisters, wives, and moms. We don't always do it right. Some of us are controlling idiots. Some of us are broken patsies. Most of us are in between, trying to do our best to make the women in our lives feel safe and cared for. It is an old paradigm. We are moving forward with the tide of society and promise not to treat women any differently than men soon. The transition will make it easier to talk about:

Abortion

Talking to other men about abortion is like transferring fortified nuclear material. Very few are engaged in the process. None of them feel like the details are theirs to share. That could be part of the problem. Men and women need to respect each other enough to find common ground. Women used to vote on issues that sent young men to war. It was life and death. Never once did we think about dividing the responsibility and taking the female opinion out of the process. It will never be an event that can be made equivalent in responsibility. Men should defer in many ways to that fact. Everyone should engage in the process of forming considered opinions and the advancement thereof.

I have to reach back to my days in Art School to find an interaction that fits this topic. The staff room never touched on the issue. My professional brush with the topic goes back to the early 2000s and it may be dated. I know that I was different in 2000. The woman was an actress in a scene I was directing. The man opposite her in the scene finds out that his younger brother was aborted. At one point in the rehearsal, she put down her script and said, "Can you imagine a man expecting a woman to carry around ten extra pounds for almost a year? It's not happening with me."

I am sure this resonates with anyone who has ever been to a casting call and been asked to lift their shirt. This was a common ask when my friends (male and female) used to go out on auditions. It makes people think about their bodies under the crushing scrutiny of the mass audience gatekeepers. It feeds a neurosis that puts the self at the center of every argument.

I understand that all abortions are good. They are all the product of thoughtful and counseled decisions. They are the only way to allow women to attain autonomy in a society that wants them chained to the role of motherhood. There is something terrifying about a baby that everyone who has had one will attest to. They make your own life and experience seem as small as the quivering helpless entity presented to you with a short wheelchair ride to an improperly installed child seat in the back of a car that is not sensible to the task of a family. It's a Mini convertible for Christ's sake. It's not a family car. I knew that for the last nine months and I didn't do anything about it until months after the birth. What is wrong with me?

Sorry for the therapy session antics. It's just a complete shift of gears in life. There is no manual. The way a father feels about life makes him ill equipped to understand the complexities of birth. There's too much love and fawning over that little life to consider the idea of losing that opportunity to be so uniquely helpless and hapless and happy.

Health is an issue. My wife was in the ICU for three days after the birth of our first son. She had postpartum preeclampsia. It was serious. Losing her would have wrecked me. So, can I understand that health of the mother has to be considered. Hell yes. Mom is the centerpiece of reproduction. If there's a family history or element of developmental danger to the mother, an abortion is on the table. Twenty-four mothers die in America for every 100,000 babies that are delivered. I can't imagine the 24 households that endure that loss. I can understand the impetus for protecting mom.

Restrictions over abortion have to be non-existent. The minute a regulation is put over the process, everyone gives up a non-negotiable liberty. The mother gets to have the final say in whether the first breath of their child is also their last. Maybe even for a cooling off period after. It's like a used car. Up to 48 hours after a car - I'm not saying that lemon laws are a perfect fit, but let's be generous to the sensibilities that align with abortion advocates. They are the only voice in the room, and they must be respected.

By Night

An actress is hardly the source for policy surrounding abortion. I mean plenty of them get pregnant from my experience with the vocation, but that's hardly a reason to take the words as gospel. It might have been the way the sympathy in the scene shifted to the male actor along with the attention. Taking attention away from any actor is like offering raw beef in an open hand to a wild animal. He might respect the boundaries between alive and dead and he may not.

The sting of what she said pulls me from my resting form. The memory transforms me into Ultra MAGA Man.

I'm not going to blow up any abortion clinics. I'm not going to scream in the faces of desperate teenage kids who see no options. I am going to engage. I am going to protect the morality of the species. We cannot abdicate matters of life and death and then expect our voices to mean something. Life is the origin of voice. It's the beginning of every gorgeous activist on both sides of every issue.

Carrying ten extra pounds? The idea of comparing a baby to fat should be a thought crime. I have no respect for the argument that vanity should be given any part of the discussion. I know that Disney makes mice into people to the delight of millions. It's part of the culture. But turning life into excess tissue does not deserve the same kind of acceptance. Simplistic answers to life and death are not helpful. The death penalty is good because there's too much traffic. I'm sure that makes sense to a sociopath on the 405, but it doesn't mean that he should say it out loud in company.

I am skeptical of abortions that occur when the child is fully formed. Any child that has progressed to the point where one has to smother his breathing or drain his cranium to stop him from becoming a viable human must have a fifty-page explanation included with the justification. Make it an even hundred. There should be a limit on how many can be performed by a single doctor. If there's one person who can find 200 reasons a year for partial birth abortion, they need to be shut down. One person per 100,000 dies due to legal abortion complications. That means people are making a safer choice by having an abortion. That should be weighed against the approximately 800,000 babies aborted in clinics across the US. How many of these people would have grown up to change the world? I know that sounds like a wide-eyed argument. Ultra MAGA Man can embrace his aspirational side too. Stop putting me into a box. Please do not make that box a coffin. Trust me. It's a bad look for abortion activists.

So, does the prospect of expecting the next step in the pro-abortion crowd to extend the time range to the undoubtedly acceptable fourth trimester abortion? It's not really a question. It is coming. The hyperbole-to-policy transition is the only thing we can expect from the modern liberal. Put up good money. You'll never be disappointed. We all have a line that we can't cross in life. It makes sense that this would come into focus when discussing the lives of viable children.

Freedom is part of quality of life. The woman who gets to make choices that would be hampered by a child does have a real point to make. Is there a way that society can ask that these choices are made before week 20? I am not asking women to regress to pre-pandemic roles in the world. We need women out there moving the society forward. Still, the Roe V. Wade discussion has to be honest. It does not make abortions illegal. It allows them to be regulated by the states. Back in the 70's, that might have been terrifying. There were republican governors who championed abortion rights in the early days. It was mainly traditional liberals who opposed the rights in the 70's. Reagan signed legislation for abortions in California while Teddy Kennedy talked about the "right to be born." Barry Goldwater was a staunch advocate for abortions. It's hard to get more OG Ultra MAGA than Goldwater. The world is not going to turn against abortions. Regional society will just dictate the rules. It's not strange that a father in Kansas might want to be informed that his 13-year-old daughter is having an abortion and a father from New York might not care at all. New Yorkers have bigger things to attend to. They have to keep incentivizing crime and violence against groups of people they don't like. Like pro-lifers?

CHAPTER 9: WAR

By Day

The week begins. I have a few extra minutes on the 405 to listen to NPR. It's the only way I can keep up with my peers. I do have to admit that advertisements every ten seconds does ruin the flow of any conversation on right-wing radio. It's steady and smooth. It's just like the well-maintained, sparsely traveled roads of SoCal. Sorry. I don't want to go there again.

War

Ukraine is crumbling. The Ukrainian flag pin business is booming. These are people who would burn the suit with the person in it if it were an American flag pin. They nod. Somber messages of fidelity. I'm actually swept up in a concept that I can actually agree with. Putin is a thug. Seeing him get a black eye would be almost worth the thousands who had to die to embarrass him. I'm still more concerned about the body count than I am the humiliation. That means I have to hide the third or fourth layer of the conversation from the others. I'm a little worried that there isn't enough conflict here to make a distinction between the MAGAs and Kashas (Keep America Shitty Homeless Aardvarks.) I know I kind of phoned that one in.

Then it happened.

"There's no way. No way he uses nuclear weapons. He's not that stupid. Push him into a corner, then crush him."

This was the statement from a lady who collects ceramic cows.

It has to be said that liberals have ramped up the rhetoric to the point of entertaining dialog. I mean that last part does feel like something the enemies of America should feel. It is said on behalf of the Ukrainians. She would probably never wish that kind of treatment against an Anti-American. I mean an eco-terrorist or invasion from the Trudeau government, just to reestablish social norms that the liberal left agrees with - that is fine. Those are acceptable lines to ignore. They are like the southern border. If something can be described as racist, the remedy is always to punish everyone who seems like they might disagree with your position. It's a wide swath, but if we're crushing people in corners, it's time to start lining up all of the enemies of the state. Unless the state is being controlled by the wrong group. Don't worry, we're working on that problem.

Crushing Putin does sound like a worthy goal. It doesn't really matter how you get to the conclusion (unless you just hate Slavic barbarians as a group in which case, it's on you) the need to get that man to take a seat is a world priority. I mean as long as that's as deep as the conversation goes, we all can join the chorus. It's disgusting that a modern human being looks at a map and slips back to 1939. These national borders are a real inconvenience to my cultural dominance of the round part of the planet.

The number of people dying in this proxy war shouldn't be part of the calculation. It's time to crush. We don't ask the orange how the pulp feels when it becomes juice. We don't even know what happens to the pulp for all of the juice that is conveniently "pulp free". Where did the pulp go? We don't know. It's not our business. We are in the business of crushing then drinking. It all gets cleaned up before the vodka hits the glass at Sandals. Don't fault the screwdriver for not completely understanding the depth of a pilot hole.

The people we lost in Vietnam are not at all like the Russian casualties being shipped back to Moscow. The scorched earth in Cambodia, where the people caught in the middle starve and burn in equal numbers, that is regrettable. Regrettable and inevitable. These people are not the victims of their home government diving into political landscapes with the idea that one more battalion will solve all of the world's problems. We haven't seen this kind of thing before. A huge misstep by the leadership class makes everyone deserving of the reprisals. Evacuate the hospitals and give the bully a roundhouse that knocks the temporal bone back into the ear canal. Crack. That will teach him.

He hasn't shown great restraint thus far, but Putin isn't crazy. He's not going to unleash nuclear winter on the world. He's quickly moving to the exit because of disease and malignant narcissism, but he'll clear up before he pushes the button. The one thing we know about Russians, is that they control their worst impulses well. I will agree that he doesn't need an excuse to do something crazy. This fog of war requires a fearless charge, not a balanced effort to isolate or negotiate. Who negotiates with world leaders who take over sovereign nations? You might tell me that's the entire purpose and history behind the public face of political science, but I don't agree. "Damn the torpedoes, full speed ahead." Admiral Farragut might have lived in 1800s, but his words are true in the land-locked terrain of central Ukraine even today.

By Night

My wife is from the UK. We often turn on the feed from her home country. The BBC has a history of reporting from warzones differently than the US. Instead of graphics and experts, they often go into the zone and talk to the people. They send back the raw feed. It's filled with fear. It's frantic and disorganized. There are no charts showing neatly stacked losses to both sides. It's bodies that still have school backpacks on them. I can't help but think that American strength might have discouraged this power grab. It might be naive, but the star-spangled bodyguard carries a big stick. The woke American progressive inspires fear in no one. One confident center of honor and order can do more for a world than a crumbling empire eating its own. It's just too self-involved to be what the world needs.

I turn into Ultra MAGA Man. I listen to the mainstream media on TV and argue with anything I hear repeated more than five times. Yes, I talk to the TV. In my defense, it's a big TV and it feels like it's being condescending.

I don't have a problem with the agenda. I quibble with the money. I really don't have the background to question tactics, but when I look at the people who designed the Afghanistan withdrawal, I do have some doubts. I'm not allowed to raise these concerns, because the world is suddenly black and white. The liberals used to mistrust the government. They used to ask questions. I want different liberals. I don't want the old ones. They were complete racists. I want the next step in liberalism. Now. The ones you can talk to and get a respectful disagreement. Putin must go is a mantra that walks a fine line. I'd be more confident if I knew the people at the top had the ability to make a plan and see it through.

The people dying in this thing is tragic. It's not just the soldiers. There are civilians who fall with every bombardment. The sick, expansionist plans of a person who is likely beyond reaching are making the streets run red. I am slightly concerned that the conflict will fascinate. It will provide profit to those in the industrial complex. It will be too important to weaken an enemy. It will not figure in the human cost on the ground. If the world decides that it has Putin exactly where they want him to be, could this cycle become a tool to use against him? What if the death of people on site serves a higher purpose in the hierarchy of global politics? That means a solution gets pushed further and further into the future. I'd take a negotiated solution today over an exclamation point that punishes the initiator. I would wait for the withdrawal and then do everything an international community could do to make his life miserable. Maybe his own people will chase him down the streets. Maybe they'll run red.

We have seen proxy wars. I hate to hit the left with this. But they are racist. They allow the local population to suffer endlessly with the goal being to teach them to be more in line with one of the parties involved. Vietnam? Korea? Syria? Which of these examples is the shining light that we're following forward? Congo? Angola? What is the model that we're trying to replicate?

If we're engaging in this kind of thing again, we'd better have a better exit strategy than EVERY past conflict that started along this model. If you're saying that it will be different this time, I'd like some examples first. Even the Russians are sending home bodies and maimed souls. Sure, they shouldn't have been there. Should have American soldiers been in Vietnam? Does that mean they deserve the hatred of the left? I would argue no in both cases. It's better to hate war than to pour an endless parade of life into the slaughterhouse and explain how the bloody chum coming out the other end is necessary. It is a sign of weakness that America is standing at this crossroads.

Putin will do whatever he wants to do in defeat. He has 80 percent approval in Russia. He treats the treasury as his bank account. He believes foreign policy is an extension of his Soviet Revival. That might sound like the worst world tour ever, and I saw Nickelback in concert. I saw Maroon Five. I am fearless, and that scares the shit out of me. Gorbachev (the last Secretary of the Soviet Union) said as recently as 2016 that he thought Putin was trying to rebuild what he had seen slip away.

Putin will give whatever order he wants to give. Guardrails be damned. People say he's dying. People say he's drank too much bleach during Covid. OK, I just made that one up. Either way, he might try to leave an impression in the history books that his people might not be able to see in the fog of war. It might leave a crater that turns millions into ash. It doesn't really matter what side of the border those things get dropped on (as always it becomes intensely personal when the discussion includes America, but let's put it aside right now) the world will be a different place when radioactive dust rates are broadcast in every weather forecast for the next 700 million years. Unlocking the atom has been the crisis that keeps on giving. It's not time to give it a reason to make a comeback.

CHAPTER 10: BAIL REFORM

By Day

Tuesday is a pretty good day for teachers. The papers that were handed in on Monday have been graded and they get returned. It's gratifying to see the youth of America finding out that there are standards. I had a kid who wrote a four-page paper ask why he failed the assignment. The paper calls for a minimum of seven pages. He argued that the mostly blank fifth page should count in his favor. I had to give him points for creativity. I didn't have to give him points for content, however. The points that go into the grade book. I've had people turn in papers from other classes then argue righteously that they should get credit.

I have to hold them accountable though. This is the English language. I can't simply give in and move them through the system. It would do them no good. It would undercut the value of my job. California is a strange place. Especially academia. People in education complain that nobody takes their job seriously. Administration has the answer. The solution is personal. I need to simply, and consistently, become more lenient. Luckily, my position is too vital for that kind of erosion of standards.

Bail Reform

There are many arms to this Kraken. And I will translate each one so that the issue doesn't present as too complex.

Criminal justice reform - Let them out of jail sooner, or don't incarcerate them at all

Bail Reform - Let them out of jail sooner or don't charge them at all

Police reform - Let them out of jail sooner, or don't arrest them at all

Sentencing reform - Let them out of jail sooner or put an ankle monitor on them and create a virtual jail that can't possibly threaten the society he or she roams freely among

It's early in the week and many of the teachers are still talking about Sunday's show by Jon Oliver. He is a very talented comedian who has the kind of cutting wit that shreds any topic he takes on. I feel sorry for those people who disagree with his monologues. He is so smart that he's figured out ways to make sure that it is absolutely clear that there is only one side of every topic. There is only one truth. It's like religion except it's funny. Super funny.

"Did you see what he did for Bail reform?" Gail never laughed, but she paused and sucked in air in a way that indicated a humorous response. Again, she did not laugh. It was really disturbing. It was like drowning in euphoria. "It was tragic." Suck in air. Suck in air. "I just couldn't stop." Suck in air. Suck.

Leave behind the idea of uncontrollable tragic suck laughter for a moment. It's pretty wild that Bail Reform is a thing. Have we thought this through? Think of all of those shows that have bail bondsmen running around collaring the rouges who skip out on their court date. Are there any people who might not benefit from freedom? Let's say somebody is accused of beating up their partner. Are there any repercussions to letting him or her back onto the street - the one on which his ex-partner lives for example? I'm talking crazy here.

It's a nonstop litany of reasons that putting cash bail into a justice system is like pouring gasoline on a tire fire. It's unfair treatment of the most vulnerable members of society. Those who have been accused of a felony. Poor people who commit crimes have to stay in jail until they go to trial. Just because someone gets arrested, it doesn't mean he committed the crime. I have seen all three seasons of true detective (yes even the second, perhaps the biggest crime against the viewing public of all time) the number of arrests of innocent people when McConaughey is present is staggering. It goes against our sacred belief in innocence until proven guilty.

Poor criminals deserve all of the respect that rich criminals get. Move them through the system through the system. There should be something like the toll lanes for repeat offenders. It would just make everything run more smoothly. Eventually, the criminal justice system might resemble the self-checkout at the store. It's insulting to assert that criminals have less honor than the 60 percent of Americans who have never spent a night in jail. There are just too many individual stories in that 40 percent. One size does not fit all. Taking money for freedom is immoral.

DA's have more important work to do than charging criminals and filling up the jails. It's incarceration nation. When you're in a hole, stop digging. If we could just push pause on all prosecutions, we would save 4.9 million lives from terrible, frankly restrictive conditions. It would free all of them to pursue something more redeeming. They have to be shown that they have a choice. It starts by giving them a one-time opportunity to get out of jail free. If that turns into a two-, or three-time opportunity, it's just the law of dynamic multiples of reform. It's still working regardless. Please stop throwing around statistics like they mean something. The crime rate is like the stock market. Everyone wins when it keeps going up.

By Night

There was a time that I celebrated fourth of July in a place that didn't appreciate my choices on how to honor the day. They were so upset, that they sent a battalion of cop cars to my location. As illegal fireworks erupted all around me, I was charged with possession of class C fireworks and asked politely to pay a thousand dollar fine. I remember that the skies were lit up with similar fireworks on every block around me. He still tore off the ticket. BOOM.

As a responsible citizen, I had to pay. It's hard to watch everyone around me not having to pay. It's like they can really do no wrong.

My MAGA Senses Tingle.

I have a hard time with the word reform. Every time it is used, it goes in the same direction. We don't reform laws to make them stricter. It's always reformed downward. I don't mind people getting more chances, or even less punishment. Isn't there a bedrock though? There has to be some base level that is the foundation of justice. If people start making fun of legal penalties, like they do grades, this country is in trouble.

The joke is always that people who disagree with Jon Oliver are intolerant. He presents it in variation upon variation of hilarious dogma. Some kid had to stay in jail just because he couldn't afford to eat that night before his alcoholic dad bet his last dollar or get medical treatment for his baby sister. I don't remember how all those points are woven together, but you'd be a dick if you even questioned that kind of narrative. It's just too downtrodden. That kid needs to get out. That kid needs to get home. There is no way to oppose the anecdotes of injustice. Worse, it makes you a bad person to think differently than the presentation leads you to. It's just mean. Well, it's also mean when people get out of jail and victimize others, but that isn't part of the narrative. Origin stories are only important with heroes. The bumps along the road might lead to a few innocents end up bloodied, terrified, or worse, but when the end goal is as pure as preserving the freedom of a criminal, that's just the kind of intolerant crap one can expect. Preach. Or maybe start with a small pilot program, learn from it, and then take the best parts of bail reform and enact them on a larger scale. Do the boring work of measuring the results. I know it's more entertaining to mock everyone who doesn't line up with the revolution, but I think that often people want boring incremental change more than they want a complete demo of lines between criminal and citizen. Or you can just keep lining up people who don't agree against a pock marked wall. It feels good being so right that you have the power to do that. It's intoxicating. Unquestioned allegiance is the best kind. And if you can force it upon a compliant population- even better.

Poor and rich people do not get treated the same. It's a problem. I am not going to mock the people who feel like their lives would be easier if they just had three extra zeros in their paycheck. Or better yet, if they wrote the paychecks and stole from the pensions of their workers. That guy wouldn't spend a single second in jail. The problem with allowing this to turn into a social justice crusade is that the mistakes are amplified by violence. Some of these people are violent. They are in jail for violent crimes. To dial up the mercy with a crowd that doesn't respect it can bring unintended consequences. In this case, it's more often deadly than any other group. So don't make mistakes with this group. Don't experiment with them. This isn't just bail; it's sentencing by judges who treat everyone like they are family. It's a nice slogan, but when murder is on the docket, I'll let Uncle Enzo burn rather than have him slashing up the yearly reunion. MAGA Man would rather have these people given more scrutiny rather than less. Ultra MAGA Man might even detain them with or without bail.

If every judge had a scorecard of the results of the people he downgraded and upgraded charges on, I'd feel better about the profession. Show me how much sympathy you have for the community by adding charges when necessary. Bust down the charges when it is appropriate. Make sure you are forced to review each of the bad decisions made. I know it's sometimes a lifetime appointment, but they should still have job reviews. They would have no bite or consequences, but the justice system should be used to that anyway.

CHAPTER 11: DRUGS

By Day

This is going to come as no surprise to anyone who has ever had conservative leanings. I'm not the life of the party. I'm socially awkward. I appreciate an adult beverage among friends, but I'm often keeping my feelings in check. I went to my high school parties with a flask that everyone thought contained alcohol. It did not. Yet, whenever I gave it to others, they claimed that they were getting "so drunk". It was a neat trick. Can we turn down the music a bit? I think we should cut Judy off. Whoa! Get off the roof. Not that way! I guess I contributed to the social scene in my own way. I have never used illegal substances of any kind. I'm that guy.

Drugs

The lamest guy in the world just got here. That's what I'd hear in my head. Even though it was my friends calling out my name over the thumping beat of another slamming party in Westminster Colorado. There were wings. Yes. I went to a notorious drug college. They handed out bongs in the freshmen welcome packet in my dorm. It was a joke, but they got used. Mushrooms were on the second floor. LSD was in the chemistry lab behind the salt. Same size container. For those of you who have worked in a science lab that's a real zinger. Trust me. Weed was EVERYWHERE. It filled up plastic bags and festered in pockets. Visine was out of stock at every store within walking distance of the campus. Heroin took more than one life while I was there. One was somebody I used to see daily. He was younger. We were casual friends. He's been gone for thirty years. Meth was a whisper in the future, but it still caught some of the "cutting edgers" and didn't let go.

"I got these new edibles from the dispensary." Reg was too

old to control the information that he relayed. It was stream of whatever conversation. He was intelligent to the degree that it got in the way of his ability to navigate the world. We would never understand Reg. He needed something to bring himself down to our level. He did this through chemistry. Never on the job. He took his work time seriously. And according to many stories. He took much of his social time in an altered state. "Look at the colors. I would, but my glaucoma is acting up." He used that joke a lot.

I wanted to know something, but it might make me look like a novice. Or even worse. I had enough empirical evidence to know that I wasn't cool. As an English teacher in my early thirties, wearing a sweater vest and tie, this might make my internal calculations public in an embarrassing way. I didn't want anyone to know. I still had to know. "How often do you treat your Cachexia?"

"Every night. It's just a glass of wine that wanders into your consciousness with an elevator to the moon."

"You ever get off in the ionosphere?" I joked. He laughed. That's what passed for humor in the department. I realized too late that he was laughing at his response before he gave it.

"Where I get off is none of your business, lad." The British accent made it several times funnier than something said in a flat American tone. I didn't know the room was listening until it erupted in laughter.

The war on drugs failed. I'm not looking for a standing army between the population and what they want. It's a waste of manpower. In fact, we shouldn't even resist the inevitable march toward comprehensive intoxication. Find a way to subsidize the things that people want most. Take the stigma (what little there is) off of everything equally. There really is no drug that should be considered too destructive (I'm looking at you Cocaine) to internal tissues or organs. We are on the verge of growing and replacing them in house anyway. Let's push the system by upping the demand. It's a win win.

Stop punishing people for a bag of weed. I've heard that up to 90 percent of the people in federal prisons are there because of a single serving of Marijuana. A brick of fentanyl? It doesn't sound any worse. It's roughly the same weight and size as a big bag of weed. Sure, it can create an overdose in 10,000 humans, but that's just chemistry and I skipped that class. I was on too much LSD. These people should be respected as businessmen. As long as they don't carry guns. Then they should be shot. Skipping into another topic.

Drug lords should be TSA pre check at very least. Stop harassing them with your prude restrictions. Look at how many medicines are shipped out by the American pharmaceutical complex. All this stuff is fortifying medicine for the intrepid "off-label" crowd. Respect the process. The people who are making these decisions of what to put into their bodies are all adults. They all have a developed idea of the consequences. They do a risk reward analysis before popping each new pill. It's a credit to the youth of this generation. They know what they are doing.

By Night

Reg is probably popping in a green right now. That's his right. It's not my business. How many kids are doing the same thing with home-pressed pills made in the back of an RV? Stop asking questions like that. It's not like you're their father. I shouldn't take on the responsibility to protect the world from, form - AAHAHAAGH!

Ultra MAGA Man emerges from the shadows of intense unaccountability. Somebody has to protect these idiots. My kids can't even put back my credit card back in my wallet after they steal it to buy online classes on investing or a gift for their mom (not a joke, my kids are something to behold). It's still on his desk as he argues that he didn't take it. This is the generation who is taking these new drugs. A sweep of my cape and I throw down on the quiet metropolis at my feet.

Treat drugs like umbrellas in the rain. Don't scream at the

sky asking for the water to stop falling. Just protect communities that need shielding. Don't open every door and throw people out into the downpour with implicit permission to soak everything in.

Structure protection is key. Keep it out of schools. Sure, some will leak in. Plug the leaks. Take it seriously. Keep it out of places of work. There was a time when every office had a bar in it. That promoted drinking in a way that we slowly realized was more of a toxic social construct. Give an umbrella to your kid when it's raining outside. Running through the rain with him or her might seem cool, but it feels like a cycle that leads to sickness, injury, or human trafficking (not sure how on that last one). What I'm saying is that it often takes them to more bad places than good.

People don't go to jail for possession of illegal drugs. If the amount processed is anywhere near personal consumption levels, it's treated like a parking ticket. That said 92 people went to jail for possession of drugs in 2017. It represented less than one percent of the people who went to jail for drug crimes.

Drugs that lead to the death of the user need to be carefully looked at. Start charging overseas producers with crimes. Set up laws that allow for legal drug production that includes standards of practice. I'm not saying a kid should be able to score a nugget of heroin at the corner store. I just want to make it safer for consenting adults and less profitable for the dickheads who push it out into the world with an AK slung over their shoulder. I know in this scenario, adopting my policies, I'm the dickhead, but drugs make for uncomfortable pairings. I'll be the dickhead who saves the world from ODs. I can live with that.

The youth of today does not handle personal responsibility well. It's our fault. We raised them. That doesn't mean we don't recognize the issue. In 2022, the new stats came in showing 105 thousand people died in overdoses in the previous year's accounting. Around the same time period (it doesn't match up exactly) 415 thousand people died of Covid. Were people twenty-five percent as worried about fentanyl as they were about Covid? They should have been. Break it down by age group and it gets worse. There were over twenty thousand deaths by OD in the group under thirty. Covid had seven. So, the young people who we protected with masks and warp speed vaccines died at a rate three times higher from opioids. Why isn't this on every newscast with contact trackers and doctors shouting contradictory messages at us every day? Young people can't take the stewardship of the modern liberal. They won't live through it to become the post-modern liberals that upset their dads. Ask any MAGA Dad. It's not so bad having a liberal kid. Losing one? That alternative is terrifying. Losing a child destroys more than one life. It drains the blood from an entire family. Ultra MAGA Man needs to answer the MAGA symbol in the sky and shout down over the rooftops. "Not on my watch."

He might not be invited to the parties, but he still can try to push back the tide of cool kids surfing into the morgue. Who knows, one of the grains of sand he saves from the battering surf, might be the next CJ Pearson.

CHAPTER 12: GUNS

What does a multi-million-dollar film producer have in common with a loser drug addict that moved in across the street from first home in a dicey urban center in Denver Colorado? Other than a crushing addiction to CNS stimulants, which an interesting overlap considering the life-trajectory each was on.

Within ten minutes of meeting them at a party, they took me aside and showed me their gun. An actual, loaded firearm in each case. It was exciting on their side. There was a real Golem in Lord of the Rings vibe about each encounter. They had something that made them special.

Guns

America is obsessed with guns. We all have one in our purse, under the visor in our car, beneath the sink. Hell, our national consensus film classic had the lead collecting a gun from the tank of a toilet. Was it Pacino or DeNiro? I can't remember.

Nobody in the teaching room has ever known anyone who owns a gun. They are civilized. They don't settle their differences with hot lead at midday. The cowboy is a static icon that belongs in the past.

For full disclosure, I don't own a gun. I live in a suburb. I did a few calculations and decided that I'd more likely shoot myself in the face loading it. I am sure that a trained individual would have much better odds.

"Can we finally just decide to get all of the guns off the streets?" Yarek knew how to make the women in the faculty room swoon. All he needed to do was take a position that clashed with his swarthy male musk and watch them applaud his defiance of stereotype.

This topic always went over the same tired ground. I'm not sure there are fresh furrows here, but I'll see if I can cut a path that helps put the California contempt in context. Maybe it will even dig a little compromise out of debate. It desperately needs something.

Guns are morally wrong. They intoxicate, but not like drugs. Drug intoxication is acceptable or better. Gun intoxication is dangerous or worse. Guns encourage people to use them. They change a normal, decent kid into a death machine. That person would never have gotten the idea to knock over the local convenience store if the gun had not been coaxing them along. This part does probably need to be investigated. I've never seen a broom that made my son want to sweep, but the allure of power in the palm of the hand probably does conduct some kind of energy. I don't think it sparks something that isn't there, but it might help a confused mind make decisions he will regret. The current circuit is causing a lot of damage. It's going to take implementation that Liberals hate to break this system.

The right to bear arms is what strict coastal constitutionalists call a typo. Sure, the first typewriter came about a hundred years after the document was produced, but that could be the reason it took so long to notice it. There is no right to own a gun. It's contraband that found a way into the system through the yokel network of chuckleheads who live in all of the states that connect New York to California.

They didn't have guns like this when it was codified. If they had, they would have certainly only given the government the right to possess them. The colonists were notably trusting of distant consolidation of power that should be given direct authority over them for their own protection. They were just done with a revolution. They saw how dangerous guns in the hands of Americans were. Americans are scary armed or not.

Finally, automatic weapons belong in the hands of trained

professionals. I am not in opposition here. I think semi-automatic rifles do a lot of damage in an urban area too. The people who scream about distinctions in this category of weapons know exactly what they're talking about however and that's helpful. Watching a librarian scream at the camera about fully automatic, grenade launching AR-15s need to be pulled from the shelves at the local Walmart really advances the conversation.

By Night

I took my kids to a gun range when we visited Utah. They had a special where you could rent unlimited guns for twenty-five dollars an hour. No coupon necessary. We shot together for the first time. It was loud. The shotgun nearly cratered my shoulder for good. I looked down and half expected that my arm had been fully removed from the socket. It might just be laying on the ground still clutching the handguard connected only by Stretch Armstrong skin. That wasn't the case, but it felt like it.

Nobody wanted to shoot the .45 handgun after my oldest begged to add it to the basket. It wasn't a cyber basket. It was literally a basket of guns we carried down to the shooting range. It was so loud that even with ear protection, I flinched every time a round was fired.

I learned that guns have a bit of a personality. My daughter's .22 was so cute. She loaded her clip by the end like an expert. I wanted to send the video to every boyfriend she ever had in the future. Can anybody teach me how to text the future? I'm ready now. Don't mess with this one. The rifle was a trip. It was the most popular gun to fire. It was easy and accurate. It got passed around. I stood watch over each MAGAzine emptied. I didn't shoot much until the end of the hour. I had to fire off the rest of the shotgun and .45 ammo. I have a pretty incredible natural aim. Unfortunately, the rounds kept bouncing off of the paper targets and not showing when I pulled them in. Somewhere after I noticed blood collecting at the base of my thumb (I'd left it too high on the grip and the slide did the rest) something about gunpowder, loud booming and blood could not be resisted. I went in a California dad. But I emerged as Ultra MAGA Man.

Guns are tools. There are a lot of tools that are being used in a way that harm others. Drones snap photos of your favorite pop icon then drop bombs on Russian tanks. Should we outlaw drones with cameras? How about with bombs? I think I'm on your side there. Accessories do matter.

If you think a computer is immoral because of hackers, then you need to have the same anger about when they are used to ruin lives. Either that or you had better find one of those horse carts in Pennsylvania. The drivers get so mad, but you will have the moral high ground. Knives are great in the hand of the butcher (unless you're a vegan that's another conversation). They are awful when on the set of a 1960's musical adaptation of Romeo and Juliet. I don't mean to get whimsical here, but if things are taken away from everyone because of the use set of an idiot, we are truly limiting society. If this tool is too dangerous to carry around in polite society, I can see some area for discussion. A set of standards that guard the most vulnerable sounds reasonable. The idea that guns are bad sounds like a children's story. Let's keep the children safe by being adults and figuring out a mature response to the problem.

The right to bear arms is real. It might not be your favorite commandment or amendment, but that doesn't mean it's not there. There is a wing of society that thinks that everything that aligns with their ideals are part of the fabric of America and those that don't need to be expunged like the statues of white men who founded this wretched place. That's not the way to get to the objective of either side. It's a way to dig trenches. Trench warfare is brutal. I will poke up my head and offer a solution. It might not work, but guns are the place that could start a greater engagement.

What if in order to collect all the guns, the conservatives got the same kind of enforcement of laws? What if they asked for the same discipline on the border? We are in a menu system of law enforcement. Each group has an appetite for different items. What if we pass gun laws, then agree that all laws that are not enforced through sentencing trigger immediate impeachment of any official not doing his job to uphold them? All the vagrancy laws in every area code. All of the gun laws in every county. It would be a different country. It is a system that barters our laws like horses in an old west boom town. It's disgusting that this is where we've gotten ourselves but lean into the parts that are acceptable and swallow the rest.

AR-15s are the boogeyman to one side and the sacred cow to the other. I don't know how to break this one down. Maybe a category of legal gun ownership that requires a year to become licensed? I know that will piss off everyone, but I'm looking for ways to deescalate this world I'm patrolling. I'm looking for solutions. Rage hasn't worked so far, so table that tactic and sit.

CHAPTER 13: GENDER ISSUES

By Day

I have to be careful introducing this one. There are a lot of emotions that attach to the issue. Most eventually land on bigotry. There is a thin slice of reason that gets shouted down every time it is introduced. I'm ready for the cascade of accusations. They say that no man is an island.

Gender Issues

There are three layers between the person who posted the following quote on twitter and the real world. I don't fault the author. He or she or xi lives in a world that elevates infamy. It's the rest of us that disgusts me.

"Look at what my daughter sent me." Callah was intensely proud of her daughter. She was a LGBTQ activist. She was living her best life and Callah was her main publicist. There was a bit of conspiracy in her voice. She knew what she was about to reveal to the room was walking up to the line.

I don't like reading twitter feeds of anyone. I am intensely interested in projector specs as they race to capture the very edges of human ability to discern detail in colors and contrast in blacks and whites. I sometimes like to look deep into the shadows of a shot in a movie that I'm watching and pretend like I'm there. I'm just not visible because I'm settled into the deepest darkest region. Anyway, I'm saying this to make a point. I don't read twitter feeds of any of the people at AVS forum. Why would I want to read Callah's daughter's feed?

I approached the computer. I stood corrected. It was less than 280 characters of - well, judge for yourself.

"For the people raising their voices against the dignity of

trans lives. I hope you get aids. Then commit suicide."

"Can you believe it?" Callah's mom asked. It wasn't just a question to me. A group had formed.

"That about sums it up." One of the educated individuals around me said in a soulful voice.

"It's a retweet." Callah's mom wanted people to know that it wasn't her daughter's thoughts. Somehow, that softened the sentiment? Perhaps second-hand suicide is more fanciful in some way? What happened next is what I'll call old people twitter. Each short comment from the faculty was spit out into the air. It disappeared with their breath. It was kind of a time-honored combination between snapchat and twitter. Without specific references to the tweet, they all made it clear that they were proud of Callah's daughter.

These were people who graded the communication skills of others. I guess it doesn't matter how inartful certain comments are expressed. The core message makes everything expressed good. A core goodness makes all tactics acceptable. So, the tenets of the Inquisition quietly push their way back to the surface. I remember how it ended for anyone who spoke up against that.

Trans lives are the only lives that deserve dignity. The youthful masses can slosh around the bottom feeders of society eating shit. They can go through the painful obstacle course we call puberty alone and ashamed. Whatever the trans people need should be delivered to them. Get rid of any obstacle they have in life. It's how white males have lived for centuries. I remember how easy growing up was for me. It was a picnic where bullies, anarchists and girls with teen spirit treated me like royalty until I was handed everything else in my life upon graduation. It is time for trans people to get the same treatment.

New pronouns are really the solution. Those old ones kept everyone back. Think how special everyone will feel when they can be referred to (as predicted in the late 18th century) as "ou" which replaces all genders. It never caught on, but we finally have the time to get back around to that mistake. It's not like the challenges of a violent, sick, attention-obsessed, and disassociated generation need to be on the front burner. If I can make just one person feel a little less awkward about being put into a gender group in conversation, then I will have made a difference today. That's honestly what has been elevated into the discourse. The goal is to avoid awkwardness rather than project merit.

There is only one way to preserve the truth of transition. The medical community has to line up behind transformative surgery. They also need to pump these kids full of therapeutic medicines designed to finally give them what they want. I knew exactly what I wanted at 14. So does everyone else. It's an insult to impulse if you question the instincts of the emerging trans life. We've seen how well liberals nurture the lives of the marginalized. Their history represents one success after another. Inner-city schools? Done. Homelessness? Tackled with kindness. Not a problem. Netflix? Any day now. Taking on something like this that affects the life course of a young individual should be done through a thoughtful, respectful process that nobody gets to question. It's the kind of thing that makes me proud of the people who know what is best for kids. That line has never been used by their adversaries. Nope. I checked the record.

By Night

I am not a social mediate. I get enough humiliation when I am asked by every third peer whether I've had my fourth covid shot. I've only had three. The minute one of them gets five, I know that I'm screwed. I can be one booster behind, and it can be chalked up to caprice. The minute I'm two behind, it's neglect, or if they don't like your activism. It's a stretch to believe that I would be a thrice jabbed fiftyish professor activist. But if they don't like you.

I try not to give anyone ammunition to have any impression of me whatsoever. Social media (among other things) spreads personality, so it is the enemy. I do not tweet, retweet, friend, or accept friends online. I used to post pictures. Everyone I knew commented on them. It felt creepy. Letting people into the personal processes of my family felt like a lie. It felt worse than that. It felt like I was craving something from others. I needed their judgement to make things more tangible. I shut it down. It felt like a sickness. I'm being told all day that it's a cure. What you think of my trans-phillic (it works, look up the suffix) daughter's activism is private. It's broadcast like an accomplishment. I feel something stir.

Ultra MAGA Man emerges. He takes a look around the internet and sneers. These people need to get a job. Absent that they need to get into the communities they champion. Do the work. Make the real relationships that will change lives. A rainbow icon is a small step. It's like an American Flag pin. Now go live a life that makes you a proud American. Be worthy of the flag. Both of them.

Kids are growing up without a compass. They don't feel like they belong in their parents' world. They aren't sure if they can create a worthy one on their own. Give them ALL support in making decisions that will lead to maturity and kindness. I don't see enough people trying to understand traditional Americans with the same compassion as they have for alternate lifestyles. That kid growing up on the farm, allowing yourself to feed your kids organic quinoa. Give him some respect too. He gets up in the morning. He listens to authority figures and then you crap upon his head like he's some kind of symbol of hate. He didn't even open his mouth. He's more polite than that. Maybe categorize him with the same compassion as you do your favorite groups. Or is this about something else?

Pronouns are language. Changing the language to suit groups of all aggrieved attention seekers could be opening the floodgates. What if the next cause is dignity for someone awful? Like homeowners? Even if it isn't, recognize that holding your breath until people recognize your special position in society warrants dismantling speech might not be the way to earn followers. Twitter followers, yes. But look at whether the alteration makes you feel good, or if it conveys goodwill on the group you're promoting. Simple slogans tend to galvanize. Complex grammar pisses people off. Ask any English instructor.

Surgery for children should be the absolute last option. Isn't it strange that this statement provokes conflict? It's a big deal. The idea that my 14-year-old self would be making decisions that would drastically change my 50-year-old lifestyle is the physical equivalent of throat vomit. It's there. It burns. It leaves an impression. Nobody in a position of authority should be pushing their ideology into the realm of transformation. I mean, the first time I turned into Ultra MAGA Man, I was terrified. I started reading slate, vox, put on NPR and BBC news in the background. I read an entire GQ, unironically. I needed to change back! Imagine it's more than spandex and a cape blocking the metamorphosis. Transgenderism has almost tripled since a 2011 study declared .003 of the population identified as transgender. I harbor no grudge to the people seeking to understand themselves. It's part of growth. It's natural. But something that might lead to 1.4 million people rushing to their doctor to prescribe gender affirming care worries me about the adult versions of these people. What if the 14-year-old is not the last word on their gender journey? It's worth considering.

CHAPTER 14: PAYBACK

By Day

I wanted to mix it up a little with this chapter. We are a little more than halfway into this Ultra discussion of culture, politics, and progress. It's been a fun ride. Instead of a topic, I want to look at tactics this chapter. I feel like the way we talk about these things might be an equal culprit in the theft of decency from the public square.

Payback

Liberals are not looking to win arguments. They are looking to destroy their opponents' lives. I've seen the playbook from the fifties. Remember when an accusation of being a communist would not only take away your job, but also your future. It was radioactive. I thought that this was something shoved into the dustbin of history like the mafia, curly fries, and physical distribution of media entertainment. What a weight off a society it would be. Instead, the left looked at the thing they hated the most and they became it. Intolerant guardians of personal destruction. Give me the bad news first. Have they ever seen a target on the right they didn't want to see a reticle over? Gun control for red states. Sniper in the tree line for the rest of us. If you don't believe me, ask: The Comedians

Dave Chappelle is not funny. He is barely a person. Anyone who goes out of their way to make fun of something like gender deserves to be cancelled. His money should be redistributed to people who warrant the bounty. His legacy needs to be a constant stream of apology over the next years. There may be some time when the grovel spectacle will allow him back at the table. Only after he absolutely admits what he did was wrong. Which joke? If you have to ask, you're watching too much Dave Chappelle. If you have to ask, you're the problem too. So shut up and let me review another heretic. I don't believe in burning people at the stake, but if it were to happen when I turned my back, I wouldn't look into the people who brought the matches.

Strangely this one doesn't believe in God, but he needs to repent in flames anyway. Ricky Gervais is old and boring. The reviewer was right. I've read five of them that tell me that his latest special is a celebration of bigotry. Joke after joke scores laughs from the kind of people that all of us have condemned categorically. British. Doesn't he have feelings? Does he have a soul? This digs in deeper than criticism of art. It asks if he needs to have his mortal soul repaired. Rotten Tomatoes currently scores his performance at 0 percent from professional reviewers. The audience score is 89 percent. Those sick people. If only they could be identified coming out of the show and followed home. I wouldn't want that, but if someone could dox them, I'd probably talk more about how much their laughter needed to be turned into fear rather than how immoral it is to do that.

People wearing red hats

Daniel Gomez Martinez got a 77-year-old veteran in a headlock and started punching in the head until he bled. He confronted evil when he saw it. I know it's easy to blame any 26-year-old in an assault case like this. But in this case, it is understandable. He saw red. Specifically, he saw the red MAGA hat on the old man's head. He and his companion told the man that they didn't like people like him before the violence began. It was kind of the old man's fault for not taking the moment to get out of there. If someone tells you that you don't belong somewhere, you'd better leave. It's in the constitution. It's an American axiom and I back it just like I back those who defund the badge.

A yard duty at an elementary school traumatized an entire school with her choice of headwear. Things that show support for a democratically elected president are still extremely offensive to those who didn't vote for him. They don't just make a statement.

They assault the senses. The aid was rightly made to call children at their homes and apologize for the hat. I think she should have been made to go there in person. This is the kind of person who should not be allowed around children again. They do that with sex offenders. This is pretty much the same thing. Just look at the quote from one of the parents who complained about the incident. "If a student is not allowed to wear a Confederate shirt to school, the aide should not be allowed to wear a MAGA hat to school." That is exactly the right comparison. Symbols of an immoral president deserve to be derided and even volunteers need to get in line, apologize, or their privileges will be looked at. There are a lot of ways a society can punish a person for voting the wrong way. There are a lot of institutions that can be brought online, not just the school.

Terrorists at school board meetings

Kids need to be masked until they promise not to infect anyone in the elite donor class. This is a hard truth, but the youth of America need to take on the chin (literally) for the squeamish quad boosted teacher class. Masks save lives. They are good for the environment. Anti-maskers have a hatred of basic ironclad virology science. And they're stupid as a bag of hammers. Parents couldn't possibly understand what the elementary teacher does. It's just a case of basic skills conversion therapy. There is a clear goal for people who complain about masks. They are vessels for ridicule. Somebody should look into it. Maybe the most powerful law enforcement arm in the country? No. They'll never go for it.

Why do parents want kids in the classroom anyway? They probably just don't want to parent. They certainly don't understand the social pressures of keeping up with the newest policies on ungrading. It's a real thing. People don't grade because grades are scary. Back to the classroom, or more to the point, yes, we said we'd go back to our jobs teaching the children when we got the vaccination. That was a framework of a plan. The head of the teacher's union called for an "alignment" of vaccine availability and going back to work. An alignment just means they're both headed that direction. It's not a promise they'll get there. What kind of grammar nerd are you to take that statement as a promise to enter a school? Another union leader said that teachers were being "bullied into returning to their classrooms." That sums it up. Stop bullying teachers. They have a contract to teach, but nobody ever said that it had to be in an effective environment. Maybe the "bullies" will try to slip that into the next contract. Until then, the school board will cut the microphone of anyone who has the nerve to suggest that they're not doing everything to get back into the classroom just because they're so convincingly not doing that through words and deeds.

By Night

Ultra MAGA Man does not like it when the weak are victimized. It just feels like hero 101 that we all need to rally behind people who are hurt by those in power. Even if the power is all in the hands of those who self-righteously proclaim that they are objectively good, and the other side is essentially evil. Nothing is that simple in this world. The hero for our time has to confront this menace. In my usual fashion, I'll do so in non-threatening prose that calls for compromise and tolerance. I'm such a badass.

Dave Chapelle is funny. He is a freaking machine. He works the room. He speaks from the heart. He cuts to the bone when he wants to and performs surgery when the subject is more delicate. People say he's the new Pryor, but I think he's the evolution of Carlin. He offends everyone in a manner that makes us all think while we're pissing ourselves. If you are offended by him, you are a humorless troll. Play the Smollett takedown on a loop until you realize that there is absurdity in all corners of existence. People like Chapelle pull these moments out of the ether and let us collectively relieve the tensions of a broken society by laughing together. Thank God this man exists.

We can't thank God for Gervais. It's not because he isn't funny. He is very funny. But he doesn't appreciate it when people bring in divinity, and I won't touch on religion when talking about him. I mean, Ricky loves talking about his balls, and he does have big brass ones! St. Augustine-sized balls. Abelard-sized balls before the gelding. Bonaventura balls at very least, and he is ready to travel with all these pilgrims. It's OK to mock his lack of faith. It makes us appreciate our own. And, let's face it, we all know Ricky would laugh if the joke were good enough.

It was devout Christians who scolded comedy in my youth. Don't make fun of God. Jesus can't take a joke. Stop assaulting the Apostles. There's nothing funny about them. Do the modern activists want to place sexuality in the same light? As I have said, there is a bit of absurdity in all human endeavors. If we shield something from inspection, we are freezing it in time. It can't evolve. It is as it will always be. Do we want people cast in that mold? Gervais talks about beating up toddlers. He then mocks the trans community. How can one statement be taken so seriously and the other laughed off? Maybe because toddlers don't have Instagram. Or maybe they just have the maturity to take a joke.

Punching a veteran who wears a hat you don't like is savage. It makes me think you need to be on a leash. You have no control over yourself when you see a symbol you don't like. Or is it because society has conditioned you to believe that you won't pay for attacking certain symbols? Vandalize a gay pride symbol and federal agencies arrive on site with tire DNA detectors. Punch a man and admit it's because you don't like the group he belongs to, and everyone looks to see if they don't like that group too before reporting it. What a messed-up protection racket. If that man was in his prime, he'd have introduced his attacker to the man who wore a uniform proudly. Violence is not the answer to the problem. Ultra MAGA Man does not believe in violence. He does believe in justice. It's up to that community to have a new MAGA hat for that man in every store and every restaurant he frequents. The kids should make drawings of him in that hat and deliver them to his house. Give the man some damn respect for being part of the American story. A story that allows people to choose who they vote for and who they respect.

Stop apologizing for being different that the douche bags who yap about symbols of hate. The balance has been thrown off so far that protecting slavery is the same as wanting conservative thought to guide the country for four years. People who love this country are not the problem. They are the ones who want to fix things. The first step is to look the people in the eye who want an apology and say simply and emphatically "No." I don't have to apologize for my ideas. Anyone who asks for half the country to be ashamed needs to decide if they hate the other half of the country or they hate themselves. I don't care which it is. I don't need to know. But for the rest of us, bring your intellect to the next session. See if you can leave your emotions at the door. A hat doesn't hurt your kids. If your kids feel hurt, you should look at your parenting. They will need to be strong enough to live in a world where people disagree. It starts by taking offense at the system that blackmails an apology from adversaries, while wearing Make-America-A-Dumpster-Fire nose rings.

New York masked kids 2-5. The clear message was that they would gladly let ideology punish the kids. Every time adults push back on liberal idiocy, they get squirrely and back away. They take their trophies in the dark. How can we get back at people who forced us back into our jobs? We'll punish the kids. The parents are distracted. They won't notice until we've done some meaningful damage. If you think a 3-year-old kid should wear a mask all day to protect himself against a disease that presents nearly zero percent risk to his future, then you don't belong in teaching. You belong working for a fascist strongman somewhere in central America. You can write his press releases. The student in Tiananmen square put himself in front of the tank. Modern liberals just line up the toddlers and cheer on the drive sprocket. It's safer to make a point that way.

Public schools are exactly what their leadership makes them. If the leadership is weak and ineffective, the school naturally progresses towards a state of stasis or deterioration. If the leadership is strong, the school swings upwards or maintains a high level. Being in class improves educational outcomes. Anyone who tells you differently is looking to make their life more convenient while undercutting the fruit of yours. It's not just teachers. Education officials seem to think that the only way to make their mark is to produce great change. It takes less work to change things for the worse than the better. People making the decisions often are self-satisfied middle managers. They take responsibility for nothing. They need to shut up their critics so they can hear the crowds chanting their praises in their own heads. They are transformational figures. Every one of them. They just need to have all of the power. That is when the system will pull out of the nosedive. It will soar. It's not about online teaching or in class teaching. It's about administration v parents. One of them gets paid for their time with the kids. In their minds, that makes them superior. Not the kind of superior that shows up during school hours in a classroom, but superior, nonetheless. The decisions made about classroom teaching is above the level of specialty of the parents. Keep talking down to the people who have entrusted you with the most valuable things they have. See if your payback on our children is worth the awakening of the beast. Do not, I repeat, do not make the moms of America angry. They aren't playing around. Just ask the dads. We are petrified of them. You think you're negotiating with a kill switch in your hand standing in front of classes full of hostages. Mom will pull out your beating heart and show it to you before pickleball with the gals.

CHAPTER 15: MEDICINE

By Day

I used to travel a lot in my youth. I have been in emergency rooms in Osaka, Chiang Mai, Kilmarnock, Moscow and, because of a state of intoxication misdiagnosed as an OD, Beppu. I've lived an unsheltered life. Some of the health crises were mine. Others were my friends. I've been to funerals (or wakes) on three continents. I have only had kids in the US. It just seemed too important to trust it to someone outside of the primary care circle. I can say with authority that America is far from perfect when it comes to medicine. I will also say that it is the best experience I have personally had. How is this a topic? Because it can never be left out of the concerns of the population. We all need medical care at some point. We want it to be superior because we're Americans.

Medicine

Ramona does not like the current system. She says often in class that the medical system in America is the best example of the way the right wing hates the entire population of the country. The party doesn't just have distaste for the masses; it wants to kill them. With the rare exception, poor people are left to die on the streets. If they can get to medical care, they can't afford the medicines they receive. If they win the lottery and get care and medicine, their employers inevitably fire them for missing work. That's what capitalism does to the medical establishment. It turns it into a tool to punish the unproductive.

Ramona is full-time. She is tenured (job security we would all welcome). She has medical insurance at one of the premier teaching hospitals in the country. Other than that, her point is well taken by the adjuncts who have no insurance, and yet they find a way to piece together enough work to cover their families with private insurance. This is a long-running show called Ramona talks about health care in the staffroom. There will be performances daily at 10:00am and 3pm. There are scattered unscheduled matinees at lunch. It just takes on anecdote about how a colleague picked up a prescription that would have cost soooo much less in Tewksbury. Where is that? It's in England. I went there for spring break. I almost WANTED to get sick in England.

Prescription medication should be cheaper. Canada. How can we be charged the kind of money we are for the same things we can get in other places? Mexico. Will someone please explain the market that exploits the sick and destitute? Somebody needs to take care of the masses. The most efficient tool for this is a governmental entity. They have performed every other task in society so efficiently, it seems like signing over twenty percent of the GDP over to them. Asking for a detailed plan first seems so imposing too. "You have to pass the bill to know what's in the bill." It's not just for today. It's the call for all medical issues in perpetuity. It's so reassuring.

Single-payer medical care will cure the system of all its ills. It's like all sicknesses: one treatment fits all. It's why we give the same drugs to cancer patients as we do to those suffering migraines. It just makes sense. If only a system developed in the rich cultural centers could be overlayed onto the interior. Everyone would thank the liberals who did it. No, they would erect statues. They would then tear down half of the statues due to the metal composition poisoning the nearby water table or because of milling deficiencies that come to light after the unveiling. The point is not having a statue. It's about having had a statue. It's the same way with government healthcare. It doesn't really matter how long it lasts. It's about winning the fight to get it passed.

Medical school should be free. Anyone willing to go through the grueling process it takes to become an MD needs the respect of a grateful society. The average debt for medical school runs around 203,000 dollars as of 2022. That's ridiculous.

It's the ultimate investment in self, and how many people have the kind of family background that allows them to place that bet? Flood the market with quality-trained professionals and the prices will come down. There is no segment of society that does not react to supply and demand. Medical demand has always exceeded capacity. See what happens if we tilt the system so that where scarcity once existed, there is abundance. It might shift the balance towards excellence, rather than just spreading basic provisions more evenly.

By Night

My wife gets migraines. Not the TV migraines where the people sit in a dark room and emerge hours later with a harrowing story. She needs to go to the emergency room. Then she emerges a day later after suffering through hell. I have been in the room when the doctor was a checklist doc and I have been there when he was a figure that took care of her the way I wanted her to be taken care of. He asked questions, listened, formulated a plan that fit the symptoms. Listened again. Did not dismiss her pain in any way. Listened a third time then made her better. I wanted to hug those doctors and hand them the keys to my car. They deserved it. None of these excellent experiences happened outside of the American system. She is British. We have been in the NHS hospitals. Impressive achievement, but the process of caring for my wife never involved the listening part. It was all about checking boxes. It's what people think they want until they cross the borders. Then the impersonal system of triage and standardized medical practices become a headache. We survived it every time, but each time I wanted more for her. I thought she deserved it. She was half-American after all.

National pride. I could feel it stir. There was no stopping the transition now. I was becoming Ultra MAGA Man. I see my country of origin as comparatively virtuous. The people are creative and innovative. NOOOO. I love almost everything about this glorious experiment. There are cracks in the medical establishment, but I think the foundation is solid.

Prescription drugs might need to be on a tiered system. There should be some regulation to all categories of medication that have no competitive production base. If one company makes a drug, I don't trust it to find compassion on the board. It's nothing against corporate America. I just think the levers of power need to be monitored when somebody is reliant on a company for life preserving care. Corporations are great at motivating people to join, make money, then die. The steps between making money and dying is not their strong suit. The bottom line shouldn't be marked with a tombstone. The people who can afford to keep the system that produces so much innovation moving forward should be charged. An income-based system that looks like the tax code might be a bit of a solution, or at least a basic strategy when taking on prescription medication.

Government healthcare would stretch resources wider without increasing the supply. It's got its own unfair properties. The middle-class has been staking the institution for years. Now, do you want to dismantle the parts they built? What did they get out of it? They grow old and get warehoused in government-run care facilities. That puts a lot on the backs of those who have paid so much to see their own standard of care shrink as they get to the age of needing it. I guess it's justice to some, but it feels like the same con they're playing with social security. Will it be there for me? If you have to ask.

I am on board with this last, slightly Un-MAGA solution. Get more people into the profession. There has to be some theater majors who might be better off with no debt and a willing audience of grandmas showing up for their rounds that might take advantage of this. Tell the world that if you want to be a doctor, you come to America. Promote the profession like they are reality stars. They get everything the world can offer them. Muffin baskets every morning before going to the morgue? Check. Free medical-grade hallucinogenics? Upon retirement, I'm fine with that. It might actually make everyone feel like the conditions are better than they really are. Two birds. Make America the center of research, innovation, and human talent development. It's not a big ask. Hey, if we're about to forgive student loans for everyone, just take the program and apply it forward for medical students. See what happens.

CHAPTER 16: SOCIAL MEDIA

By Day

Let's take all of the aspects of human life and put them online. It will strip out all of the base impulses. It will push us forward into a new world that carries none of the annoying effects of the last. We will not be violent online. How could we? I've played video games. Those characters are all just fine even after they are ripped apart into bloody pieces. Why are we drawn towards that part of conflict? That's another conversation.

We will leave the dishonesty of the real world behind. We will be forthright. We will be our true selves. Our profile pictures will be the badge of honor that we are human.

What good would stealing be in cyber space? There's no such thing as crypto currency. We are safe the minute we hit this new digital plateau. The world will open up below us with none of the characteristics of the last. We bring our new selves to this land. It will be the most beautiful expression of what humanity can be.

Social Media

Living online is basically taking the sewer line and redirecting it back into your house. It is all of the ugliness of the human form amplified by access that transcends bankers' hours. It leaves us as a quivering in muck, a smelly mass of neuroses. We have taken the spigot of humanity- turned it up full force like a fire hydrant - then told everyone to drink from it. It is messy in ways that even someone who doesn't live in both worlds can recognize.

"I haven't been on Facebook since I recognized how little authenticity it promotes in users." This was my comment to the blonde Aussie who asked why I hadn't yet accepted her friend request. It had been 48 hours.

In my defense, I hadn't logged in for four years. I was going backwards. That's what many of my progressive colleagues said. I would rather install a landline in my house. I bet he still has an aol.com email. Do you still use Netscape Navigator to get to Ask Jeeves? I push the good-natured ribbing aside.

"I only joined in the first place to please (and I still can't believe this) my mom."

"So, your mom is more technologically advanced than you are?"

"I didn't say that."

I don't have time to explain my regression theory on the metaverse. I don't have the energy to stand up to a majority. It feels like the fifties and I'm the only non-smoker in the room. Do I know that cancer is coming? No. I just hate the smell. Same with Twitter. I don't know how it will damage me, but I just feel like it will blossom like Foxglove. And it won't be the kind of shift that can be remedied with something simple like death. It will be that immortal demon we awaken into our culture. It will prey on the children of our grandchildren. We're just in stage one. Wait until this really gets rolling.

It's a revolutionary tool. Progressives love revolution (when it's going in the right - read left -direction). Ruth Sent Us can predict what Ginsburg wanted from beyond the grave. It can be sent as a tool of change to protest a decision that hasn't been made yet. This sounds like science fiction, but it's just good governance. Stay ahead of your opponent. #8cantwait can change over a weekend into something that makes sure that no policeman ever points a gun at an individual who does anything to anyone. We can't make that decision. Ruth, she needs to be heard. But the police need to be shut down. Hashtags can be the way to get everyone talking about your cause. If enough people show up, whatever they do can't be wrong. It's the oldest power play in the book. Outnumber the enemy. Social media isn't a threat to anybody except the people who deserve to be threatened.

Organizing a riot that punishes a middle-class community for the actions of an inner-city police officer in Chicago makes sense. It just clears the bar. Don't ask how. Letting everyone speak in an open forum - that doesn't pass the sniff test. What if someone makes an argument that those in power don't like? That sounds like it might be something that needs to be policed. "A place that needs to be policed?" you ask. The border? No. Cities? No. The Capitol? Yes. Thoughts? Yes. Keep that straight. Important things are being done in the capitol. They can't be interrupted by troubadours of insurrection. Those people were serious. They could have killed somebody. They didn't, but they could have. The only person killed was a woman, Ashli Babbit, who was caught in a place she shouldn't have been. Like Breonna Taylor? No. She was killed in sinister crossfire. There is righteous and sinister crossfire. We need somebody on the internet who can keep this straight for everyone. We need a new governmental body tasked to keep people thinking about the right things (read left). If only everyone who understands the aims progressive policies could redact, edit, republish, and put their thoughts out into the world, none of the problems we are having would ever be heard of. Think how much easier it would be to plan a future perfect world, if you weren't concerned with the details of the misery your program is inflicting upon the now.

There is a serious, "always on" issue that social media is having on our kids. This is something that I think both sides can find some kind of common ground upon. Imagine a compulsion to live online. Now imagine that online space is constantly telling you how much your life is complete garbage. I believe this is the state of being for most of the idiot oddballs I called friends in high school are living today. We were not cool. I read a lot. They juggled, snorted aspirin, and drank wine coolers because beer tasted bad. These people were virulently nerdy, but we managed in a small community in kind. We supported each other because we knew how much the rest of the world was out of step with our own special brand of awesome. We heard from our peers during school hours only. And since most of us were in show choir, we didn't even have to experience all periods with people who might judge us. Add in band class and there was a third of the day where we were untouchable.

By Night

I reached out to a friend after finding his email address in an alumni announcement. He was living on a commune. Talking on the phone made me want to see him. We laughed and made plans. He didn't mock me for suggesting we actually meet somewhere. It was the kind of comfortable that made me think about how nice it was to be able to put a hand on the shoulder of somebody who had earned your trust over years of close contact.

Kinship with humanity. I felt myself changing. I tried to put down the phone because my buddy is about as liberal as a hippie who makes his own soap can be. I didn't want him to hear me change. "I've got to go. Fuck Trump. Actually, the guy wasn't that bad - " I hung up on myself before I could push the blade into the relationship any further. He did call me back. But he never mentioned the way we signed off. Ever.

Every hashtag that leads to violence and destruction of property deserves to be investigated. Do the organizers need to have their virtual heads on pikes at the gates of the internet? Probably not. I would line up everyone who caused the damage into a battalion that has to clean it up. I'd have them talk to the people who they hurt as they pushed forward with their version of restorative justice. They would need to make the people who they harmed whole. That's what they're seeking for their own causes. It's the least they can do to expect the same of themselves. What if somebody dies? That might be what they're protesting. You're never going to make that right. You carry that with you. It's not just the move of some bad actors in your revolution. You don't like that argument when it's against the police. Start reforming your group the same as you want the police reformed. Do the work to make your internet mob into something that society can count on to do the right thing. It's really what both sides want. Place the guardrails on the left and right. It works better, especially when you don't know for sure which side has the cliff on it and we're running down a dark road.

For every edit the left wants to make to a post, the right gets to make one too. Nothing gets posted until both sides have their 280 characters on each issue. That's the way to make censorship fair. Does that sound tedious? It does to me. I'd just rather have every idea expressed by the people who have them. It gives people a good picture of the world as it exists. It's not pretty, but that concealer you're asking for is just a way to catfish the plurality of voters. Eventually, the morning after the election, you're going to wake up in a bed with somebody that looks a lot like the people in the English Department of every college I've ever been to (we are notoriously unattractive specimens). It's not going to make anyone happy. It's just going to make everything look fine until it isn't. That transition can be revolutionary or incremental. People usually stay alive better when it comes in small movements that correct course. Only flat Earthers think we are sailing off the edge. Live with the other side getting a say in the direction of the country and just win the argument by degree.

American teens are living in a world of non-stop peer pressure. I could barely handle the allotment that I got, so I can't imagine they are dealing it with it any better than I was. I turned to musical theater. Yes, it was that bad. I know the American songbook backwards and forwards. It's pathetic (that other people don't). It was reported in 2019 that 30 percent of teens experienced bullying more than once online. Since kids always lie, I'd put the real number at somewhere north of 100 percent. Maybe more. If even thirty percent of teens were smoking, there would be a council that met daily to handle the national health crisis. If thirty percent of teen women got pregnant more than once - other than having an adorably chill baby boom - we'd have daily briefings on how condoms can be worn all day just in case and women can get a mobile abortion during passing periods. I am not being that glib. These are numbers that scare people who see how much can change with just a small cross section of humanity. It doesn't take a majority to change the character of American youth. On the other hand, youth are resilient. They live through wars and genocide, then become the greatest generation. I'm not sounding the alarm. It's more of a dog whistle to those who want some innocence left in their children. Find a way to limit anything toxic in their lives. If that's cigarettes, sex, drugs, or social media - all are addictive substances that might need to be put on hold until adulthood. And to the adults out there, have sex, a pack of Marlboro reds and a fifth of Jack Daniels. The data is in. It's better use of your time than spending your day on Facebook.

CHAPTER 17: THE BORDER

By Day

There is nothing that opens the mind like travel. Not just the kind that has tailored activities, schedules, and itineraries. In my youth, I was the kind of person who got on a plane without a return trip booked. I found it very satisfying. I have lived in three countries. I also spent six months in Utah. I'm not sure how you count that. It feels almost like another country after you live in California for a while. One learns many things that one doesn't want to learn. I discovered that buses in Indonesia slid off the "road" on every other mountain turn. I found out that a place that looked like tea house in Kyoto was really just a residence with a sleeping man in the front room. He has a story for life. I discovered why Russians are so pissed off after walking through Moscow in January searching for a place to buy a towel. Russia has the kind of cold weather that feels like a grudge. It is downright abusive. We all know the immaturity abused children exhibit on the topics of borscht and global conflict.

They tend to get cross. So does our next construct.

The Border

We draw lines on maps all the time. Some of those lines are very important. Longitude and latitude have guided sailors since Hipparchus standardized the global system in the second century BC (I know there are some Eratosthenes fans out there who will clamor that his work was the origin of the system but give me a break. I mean lines that bend into major cities? It shows a Egypto-centrism that is truly repugnant by modern standards.) Sometimes the lines make sense. Sometimes they do not. How is it that the US still has Point Roberts? Can someone explain how Chile and New Zealand have smaller claims on Antarctica than

Norway? Proximity justice activists are going to go crazy when they find out.

Russia shares borders with 12 countries. China tips the scales with 14. The US only has two. And yet, we find a way to turn both into chaotic truck parking lots and human traffickers candy land. Order and chaos are in sharp contrast in this argument. It's probably the one issue that sets up the standards of both and how they align with political policies. But it feels like we're always get distracted.

"The republicans are just worried they are going to lose their privilege. Borders are immoral." This was Katya. She was a white female whose parents fled the Soviet Union a generation ago. I saw an opening.

I added. "There's also an element of sexism in it as well." The room murmured approval. It didn't matter that it didn't make sense. How was this a male and female issue? I had no idea. I just knew how to get approval. I might need it later when I asked for a day off to protest (I was really going fishing, can't say that).

The room was primarily white. The room was 70/30 female to male. The full-time staff were all white. All of them. Not a single brown person. The girl from Iran? She was part-time. The woman from Guatemala? Part-time. Were there any African American people who could join the teaching staff? Not one. These people had built their tree fort in the back yard of their parents sprawling suburban house and they let nobody into the club except the people they decided worthy. None of those worthy people happened to have pigment. But they stood on the balcony, shouting to the wind that exclusionary clubs were the tools of idiots and bigots.

America benefits from unlimited migration from a perpetual underclass. There are people in the world born to be on the bottom rung of society and we need to invite them into the country to shoulder the burden of the labor that makes prosperity available to a compassionate, deserving society. They do the jobs that Americans don't want to do. That's the lesson for the ages. It's been repeated by Republicans and Democrats. Our population can only be catered to. They are not up to the daily maintenance. Why should they be? They are the deserving inheritance class. Ask anything more from them than those expressed by their inner desires to be their authentic selves and it's a thought crime. Ninety percent of garbage men from my generation wanted to be astronauts when they were kids. Now, ninety percent of the astronaut aspirants are playing video games while somebody named Doug from Canada empties their trash. Surplus astronaut trainees are a sign of progress.

Imposing order on the process is the kind of thing that leads to mean judgements about who deserves to come into the country and who does not. Who are we to judge whether a person has a claim of refugee status? They're all refugees from their countries. These are terrible places. Have you been to Ottawa? It's a nightmare. A very polite nightmare. There is nothing condescending to say that all other countries citizens deserve entry based on the barbaric disorder of their home countries. Making laws that allow this process is not the answer. It will take too long for democracy to come around to the needs of the people. We have to simply swallow the bitter pill that there will be some mistakes when we rip up the rule book. Nobody will take advantage of this lapse of the rule of law. It's too decent of an idea. We are the north star in a post-pirate world.

Keeping children in cages is the image that defines conservative America. They invited them all up here, and then they decided that their insatiable hatred for children (don't look at abortion right now) had to be expressed somehow. There was only really one way forward. They had to put them in cages. These measures were drawn up and approved by the republican leadership class. It goes all the way up to the president. Who do you think designed the cage? It was on his first day in office. The pictures were under a different president? One we liked? Well, never mind, Obama put kids in cages as a last resort. He tucked them all in every night he was in office. So, intention plays a big role in how the cages are perceived.

By Night

The media is a modern protection racket. Both sides, but since most newspapers haven't endorsed a republican since continental drift was in its infancy, I'm willing to point out the scales have fingerprints all over them on the left. As hypocrisy hangs thick in the air, I take a deep breath. Ultra MAGA Man emerges from the cloud. Am I an angel? Probably not. Am I a superhero for the downtrodden? I do my best work with the downtrodden. I am an enemy of the uptrodden. Those elites have had the microphone for too long. I feel a voice long dormant awaken.

The United States cannot make up rules about immigration each time the presidency changes. We need to agree on some policy. It needs to be put into law. That law needs to be enforced. I know there are laws right now, but they are not considered anything more than guidelines by the resident of 1600 Pennsylvania Ave. Pulling up a workforce from another hemisphere is not the answer. The only way to fix this is to have all Latinos vote Republican. I can see the future. It's going to happen. The people who have fled chaotic governments want something stable for their kids. They deserve order. So do the rest of us. So, please Latino culture, find your inner conservatives and help the aging culture of America welcome in a diverse generation with rules and standards that lead to safety and protection of those who are most vulnerable.

Calling everyone a refugee is insulting. People seeking opportunity should not have to lie. They should be given a chance to apply for a visa. They deserve the dignity of knowing that they will be welcomed in and that those who want to break the laws of America will not get better treatment than them. A generation from now, the border will be lasers and robots detaining drug smugglers. Before this transition into orderly border authority, or dystopic hellscape depending on what side of the law you are on, we need to make decisions that preserve the standards of how we treat our fellow man. Coming to your front door deserves a very different reaction than breaking in through your side window. If we can't find a way to invite people in by a lawful process, everyone is going to lose trust in the system. The left hates nationalism but wait until the flag means nothing to anybody. That's a world MAGA Man can't imagine. And it probably isn't one worth living in.

Using an image of a child to elevate a political cause has a deep, rich history. It's not always manipulative. It is always emotional. It drags us into a world where a child deserves poor treatment. Nobody likes that world. I understand that reminder. It's important to think about how much children bring to the world. If we don't have a world to protect, we often turn bitter, internal, and liberal. Sorry for the shot, but I don't meet many of my child-bearing peers who believe that it's fine to encourage migration of unaccompanied minors to prove a point. Then, when it turns out it was your man in the office, you barked about how it didn't matter who was in charge, it was the local application of the law. It was the border that was immoral, not the way it was used to advance a political agenda. The value of human life can't come down to an argument between us and them. One child face down on the banks of the Rio Grande is one too many. Stop pushing a system that invites tragedy like that. Reform the system into something that welcomes that child through a litany of painful compromise on both sides.

CHAPTER 18: RACISM

By Day

I grew up in a sheltered part of America. There was very little racial division. The largest minority (bend your mind around that) was Native Americans. The white kids treated these "Indians" with ignorance and reverence. They were cool because many of the boys were much better at sports than their depigmented brethren. I'm sure it didn't make their lives any easier busing in from the reservations. We acted like that didn't happen. It was a form of treason by modern day standards, but so were many of the things said and done in the 80's. The good news is that people of good faith have made it better for my kids. It will be better for the next generation too. But bringing that up is the same as ignoring the original sin of:

Racism

"These people make me sick." Deborah was holding up a newspaper. Was it a murderer? Was it a Wall Street raider who took the retirement of countless grandmas so that he could live in a world with just another decimal point moved over? No. This was a kid in a MAGA hat. A Native-American was playing a drum in the edge of the frame. "He looks so smug." Well, all men look smug when they're happy. They shouldn't be happy. Especially white men. What right did he have to accost that poor old person of color?

The worst thing about that picture is that it urged everyone to take sides. There was one race that was good, and the other that had motives that everyone was expected to question. They were not urged to question the situation, the context or what happened up until that moment or after. Just look at the skin. It tells the story. That's not racism. I've been assured. It's an honest mistake when it goes against orthodoxy. Somehow, this is an acceptable excuse when offered by one side, but not the other. Progressives deserve it. They've earned it. They were the ones who steered southern politics to disrupt the Republican reconstruction efforts with 4 million of their friends in the KKK. Three members of congress served proudly as members of the KKK. All three were democrats. The benefit of the doubt just skipped a generation or two in this case. Now, it's back.

It is right to call your political adversaries racist. It's a moral imperative to make sure that people who disagree with you are labeled as such. How else will people understand how wrong they are? It's like the f-word. I grew up hearing it once or twice in hushed tones. Now, it's everywhere. I think my grandma said it last week. This is the evolution of calling somebody a racist. Proof is for the nerds. How do you disprove racism when you oppose progressive policies? The same policies that have kept inner city black communities on the lowest rungs of American prosperity for decades? Those are the ones. Turn on the news. These are the smartest people in our public sphere. They have the looks of an actor and the limited skill set of a prompter reader. They are like politicians that come into our house every night with ideas predigested for the masses. They deserve respect. They have been noticing a lot of racism in their political enemies. We have to take them seriously.

Black people can be racist when they align their thoughts with the wrong element. They just don't know what's best for them. Assault Larry Elder in a gorilla mask and it's just fun. The old trope that he is a monkey, or some lesser species, is the kind of joke that the left can make without accountability. They serve his community. He just can't see the progress. It's more of a lack of vision in Black people who don't vote with liberals. They are missing part of themselves. They are just less black. And worse they've replaced that black part with something more akin to whiteness. Since white people, see the skin comment earlier, are the root of every problem, it's only right to inform them in a public forum. They just aren't acting black. It's fine. We will wait until you come to your senses. Please do so before we have to ruin your life- for the betterment of black people.

There is never progress in race relations. Pockets of racism are the exact thing as pervasive public racism. In fact, they might be more pernicious because you have to go looking for them instead of seeing them out in the open. The time it takes to discover racism should be taken into account. There are so many proud racists in our society. America protects and amplifies their voices. Look at the public statements of republicans. They are laced with racism on every level. I mean, you have to read in some pretty malicious shit to interpret it that way, but I have the authority to do that. I'm a proud Californian. I know racism when I create it from the whole cloth spouted from the people I hate. The people I hate. That has a nice ring to it. I really should attribute that to a whole group of people. Nothing bad can happen there.

By Night

I just realized that I dropped the daily routine thing. It was probably getting boring anyway.

I was in a bowling alley. It just happened when the ball struck the pins. A concussion of laughter, comradery and community just pulled on my reigns. Everyone was talking about the photo. I'd learned context in the interim that I wanted to share. NOOOO! I stumbled into the parking lot so that nobody would see me turn into Ultra MAGA Man. My wife appeared at my elbow.

"You were about to say something that would lose us friends."

"Family, too." I added.

"Let's get you home." She moved me to the car. In that moment she was the hero. Ultra MAGA Man needs to have Super Incredi Woman by his side. Who else would get him out of trouble time and time again?

Can we stop introducing race into every argument? Roads are not racist. They are symbiotic accessories of mass conveyance. In California, they do have a bit of an attitude, but that's another topic. Are there racist people on the roads? I'll cede that possibility, but make sure you have someone engaging in racist rhetoric or behavior before you pull that lever. Pit bulls are considered racist by the Baltimore Sun. No. The reputation of a dog cannot be compared with young black men without such ignorance and contempt for the men showing through. Men are not dogs. Hiring practices have racism laced into the process. The favored class always get benefits in the interview process. Harvard did a study where they sent out identical resumes for two people: Greg and Tyrone. Guess which one had to wait an extra two weeks for an interview? Now, this might just be about how comfortable HR is with people with different names. Would a Russian name get the same disfavor as a traditionally African American name? I don't know. But this is the place we need to address the struggle of all races. Make them welcome into the workplace where they can excel. It will do much more for them than calling the roads along which they walk their pit bulls racist.

Black republicans are not racist. They are part of the diversity of thought that everyone who has taken place in the great American experiment has aspired to. When Candice Owens blames social problems in the Black community on liberal policies, it might be because that's what she believes. She might be an intelligent black woman who came to a different conclusion than others of her race. White people are allowed to think a myriad of things. We actually believe deep down that dentistry is a respectable profession. Messed up, but true. White Americans have the privilege of having their ideas attacked without mentioning their race. It's like our thoughts can be considered without the addition of pigment to the argument. Thoughts in a white person are thoughts. Thoughts in a black person are black thoughts. I wonder if black physicists do black physics? Or if black doctors practice black medicine? I'd think that would be pretty damn insulting to their education and process. But I guess it's ok if you have nothing of value to say about the content of the thoughts. If you know nothing about wine, talk about the design of the label. Maybe nobody will notice.

There has never been a better time to move race relations forward. People are listening to every ethnic minority. Groups are not being dismissed because of their skin color. Find one news article that promotes hatred of a group of people based on their origin (unless you're talking about academic origin- Yalees are subhuman at best- you heard me Yale - suck it - and I'm not just saying that because I didn't get in - this is a fair condemnation of Yale and all of its sinister alum) and I'll show you an unhinged fringe player in the public discourse. Noticing that people are gaining respect for everyone in a multi-ethnic society is not an ugly truth. It's the basis for hope. Disney has black princesses. Netflix has Latinx leads. And inclusion that doesn't stop at race, we have a president who displays multiple mental handicaps and people barely even mention it. It's inspiring. We've moved beyond fear and exclusion in many sectors of American life. Don't be afraid to notice the good as we crusade against the bad.

CHAPTER 19: FOSSIL FUELS

By Day

I have one car that takes gasoline. It gets 35 MPG. I got a hybrid before they were cool. I bought an EV before they even knew how to make batteries (thanks GM). I stopped using Vaseline because it was petroleum jelly. I much prefer smearing my lips with avocado butter. Fair trade.

This doesn't mean that I hate oil. It means that I prefer to make choices that cost me a premium to be on the right side of the carbon balance. Awareness is not a noose around the neck. Adaptation is not a suicide pact. We can be reasonable even when it comes to:

Fossil Fuels

The evil fluid. A slick wet obscenity. There is nothing that can be done to change it. It just comes out of the ground bad. Sure, it's natural. It's organic. How can I explain that coal is bad organic material and acai berries are good organic material? I know.

"Did you see that gas is seven dollars a gallon?" Derek is such a tool. He didn't even see it coming. I almost lip synched the response (with avocado shine on my lips).

"I hope it goes to ten dollars a gallon." It used to be nine dollars a gallon, but hyperbole has to rise with inflation. The next comments were less on script, but still predictable.

"It's good."

"Let them suffer."

"These people are killing the planet."

"They're destroying the air quality."

"Everyone should be on the bus."

None of them take public transportation to work. Not a single one. One of the old-school grammar teachers walks three blocks from her apartment. But she has a car, and it shows up parked in the handicap space just outside the office on "lazy" days. I should be with them. Everything about my lifestyle screams that I am on board. Maybe Ultra MAGA Man has finally met his match?

Carbon fuel is dead. Not just dead creatures decomposing over centuries. I mean dead in the way that bell bottoms are dead. The way that hippies are dead (Oregon excepted). The way that scorches the earth just below the sedentary layer and means it will never come back. Carbon fuel is the Detroit lions of energy. Relegated to the point nobody even remembers what they're doing on the field. Stop drilling. Stop moving it around the planet. Enter trade agreements that immediately cuts off the spigot here and on the other side they promise to stop drilling the minute it stops being profitable for their country. Soon. They will promise to consider it soon, and that's all we can really ask for. Fracking should have a mandatory jail sentence for using the word. It's an ugly word. It's an ugly business. Get the oil platforms off of my ocean. Drag the boats back to port, except for the ones who have virtuous owners who are going to a climate conference on their yacht. Not completely on their yacht. They take the helicopter in when they get near the shore. They're not animals.

Trucks need to stop using diesel immediately. A mass conversion to battery power is henceforth the rule of the land. There will be some small disruptions in the supply chain. People will starve, but as they embrace the blackness, as they are headed for their own conversion into inert elements, they will thank the people sitting down to brunch (after almost 50 minutes of a wait) who made the sacrifice in their stead. These are the people who want it the most. They know that the price of bread is secondary to the temperature in the arctic shelf projected forward thirty or forty years. Or maybe only ten. Think about that. In ten years, that person might have drowned. He really owes the activists who pulled the pin on this grenade now in case the enemy attacks at dawn. It's prudent thinking. It's what anyone who cares about the plight of the poor would do. Squeeze them until you feel better about their future. They will understand. The planet needs us now. The people on the planet will forgive us later.

The only way to make people change to renewables is to raise the price of fuel and natural gas. Hit grandpa in the wallet every time he wants to heat his house, and he'll put solar on the roof come spring. It's really their fault for not embracing change willingly. There is no other way. Natural gas prices have tripled over the last calendar year. It's the stick that will get people off their lazy comfortable asses and propel them into the Green New Deal. The carrot is overrated. It needn't even be tried. They had their carrot time. Petroleum products took about forty years to take off from the first wells in America in 1859. The sunset should be compressed to five? Yeah, five sounds right.

Wars have started over oil prices and production. That was the old world. No aggression in the past year or so has had anything to do with energy. Well, maybe one. The point is that quick moves in the industry do not have any historical danger associated with them. Ten state-sponsored armed conflicts tops. Casualties of those wars? Don't think about the process. Think about the goal. It is to keep the planet alive. Considering how many times the planet has died over just the last few billions of years - this is brinksmanship at the very least. We don't have time to think about consequences when talking about oil.

By Night

My car glides silently into the garage. I've decided to do the right thing. I'm going to get rid of all petroleum products in my life. It's the only way to deescalate the stand-off between humanity and the environment. The tipping point sounds so final. I mean, planetary extinction is the least of our worries if I am to believe Penny Whetton. The bigotry of my misconceptions of what a walkabout really is might require instant dingo-based subclavian extraction. Bloody right it does.

So, here it goes:

I start a pile. Cassettes? Easy. Wasn't using those anyway this century. Golf bag? The water requirements alone make me sick that anyone who engages in this as recreation. So far, so good. Caulking? I kind of like a neat backsplash, but sacrifices must be made. Dice, rope, lotion, toothbrush- this is beginning to hurt. I'll find a substitute. Sunglasses, refrigerators, golf balls (how does this hurt more than the bag?), toothpaste, pillows, deodorant - then I come to a crisis of conscience. My football. The pigskin has to cover a nylon air bladder. The same bladder that Brady either did or did not deflate on the way to becoming the greatest QB of all time not named Manning. Give up football? I throw up a little, irrigating my nasal cavity before draining into the back of my throat. I spin the ball in my hand.

Ultra MAGA Man intercepts. I am flooded with crude thoughts. Couldn't help it. I shouldn't fix the world like a toddler. I am not going to hold my breath until I get my way. I can't do it like a teenager. The carbon economy is not the poison that holds no compromise. It's not an immediate choice between life and death. I am not a carbon traitor or trader. I view this crisis in a nautical way. A responsible hand on a till, that will guide the world forward. Standards and course will change slowly until one day, the problem that seemed so all or nothing will be a struggle at the margins. It will no longer be the existential crisis on all cycles of mean solar time ending in Day.

Nearly 77 million barrels are pulled out of the ground daily. Every dairy cow produces a barrel of milk every three days. There are 270 million dairy cows in the world. If the math holds, that means 90 million barrels of milk a day. I'd like to shift the way we look at this problem. It's just swapping out one liquid for another. Simple. There are two ways to address a problem like this. Kill all the cows today (it can be done) and then figure out the solution on the other side of the decision. It would work. It's like asking for forgiveness rather than permission. The problem is that you're playing with the diet of about 150 million food-insecure children in the world. If it's worth it to put that many people in danger, then do it. Please don't talk about the nobility of your crusade. It's a choice of two evils.

Same thing happens when you cut off fuel. It's not like the planet suddenly became hospitable to the unaltered environment surrounding the human condition. People with freeze. There will be short or long period where the world has to problem solve. The weakest members of society will be the grist in this period. They will be ground down into their least prosperous form, even if that is inert. It will be dry and bloody both in the same breath.

Trucks that convert to battery will also pull 9 in ten people out of the fulfillment business. They are going to replace people when they replace the power source. The writing is on the wall. Autonomous driving vehicles will be part of the trucking revolution. There are a lot of people who are afraid of losing their livelihood to this transition. Don't mock them. It's hard to hear that your identity is not valued where you live. It's not something that Ultra MAGA Man has struggled with. I'm stronger than that. But it would be difficult to tell a group of people who kept the country running for a century that their wealth was about to shift into the tech sector. Have fun chasing after that in re-training.

How does everyone feel about Russia being a major trading partner in the global oil market? Saudi Arabia? Iran? One has killed between 4-6 thousand people for being gay. One still thinks that crucifixion is a great way to send a message to those people who aren't beheaded or stoned. One believes that 30,000 of their own soldiers can die for a reunification plan of the old CCCP that doesn't require a basis in rational thinking. What was it again? There are Nazis in Ukraine that need to be put down by a foreign army? Clear. Chrystal. That same country gave Stephen Segal citizenship. Another war crime. Every plan that calls for America to cut production gives more power to those in the global gas station cabal. They are not known for their restraint or progressive policies. If we want to have these people in leadership, then we should give them the power of the free market.

Otherwise, we have to drill into the ground and pull as much power from it as possible. Do it in a way that is cleaner, better, and seeks to make every week peak oil in the world. Behind it can come the engineers and environmental paradigm disruptors that will fuel their innovation on the back of profits from the industry that they will some day bankrupt. It will be the most beautiful irony that they get there faster when our oil industry is the best in the world.

CHAPTER 20: COVID

By Day

We are two years past the pandemic. I have three shots of Pfizer in my arm and a shot of Jack Daniels in my stomach every night. I have done everything society has asked of me. Even when it feels like it might be verging on ridiculous. What does that look like, you ask?

Well, I recently went to see a production of Into the Woods at a local community college. Sondheim was not in attendance. He had died a few months before this production. This is important later in the story.

We took our seats. The auditorium was a little bit awkward. Even though everybody had put the fear behind them, there were still places where the thought of large crowds combined with two years of justifiable fear led to mild background social anxiety. Was it a good idea to be among so many people? They might be infected. They will almost certainly be breathing during the entire show. Nobody was maintaining a strict adherence to a mask policy. They'd stopped that in Fall semester. Eight months of the wild west. People breathing everywhere. Flaunting their bare lips like they were on the catwalk in Paris.

I know the build-up is a little too much at this point, but I can't back down. Like Kim Petras' new version of Kate Bush's classic song Running up that Hill teaches us - there is always a bargain when seeking contentment. It comes only after the effort that both build us up and destroys us at the same time. That was what I was about to watch unfold in front of me. The PA system crackled to life.

"Today, the actors were informed that there was a close contact trace to one of the cast members, so they will be performing in their K-95 masks. Enjoy the show."

The exits were so close. I would have to leave behind my wife, child, and sundry other professional associates I had come with, but I could make it. My wife mouthed the words "save yourself." Unfortunately, that extra moment doomed my flight. The house lights dimmed. The actors took the stage.

If you've never seen Sondheim performed underneath the confines of five-layers of surgical protection, I'd give you this comparison. Cup your hands in front of your face. Keep your fingers tight together, then sing into that enclosure. Sing anything. It won't matter. Try to match pitch, or worse, harmonize. I dare you.

The title of the show is Into the Woods. I don't think that anyone even recognized the words of the chorus. The jokes fell into a jumble of sounds that could be compared to a bucket mute solo on a trombone. There was a moment at the end of act one where the Wicked Witch is supposed to come onto stage in a sparkly dress and announce that a curse had been lifted. Unfortunately, there was no way to tell she had been old and ugly under the mask, so the "transformation" was more of a costume change without decipherable explanation.

I grew up listening to Sondheim music, and I would never have wished him anything but health and long life until I saw that production. I was glad, as I exited during the act break that he didn't have to be there to see what the department of public health in conjunction with the CDC and state of California had done to one of his works.

The air was fresh and crisp as I walked away from the auditorium. It felt like there was nothing in the world that could make me uncomfortable again. I had witnessed the Everest of ignominy. I could draw upon a source of strength that few could even comprehend. My powers were emerging. I was almost a true superhero. I now needed a supervillain. Something new. Something that nobody sees coming.

Covid

It was just past two years into the pandemic when a particularly strident English teacher took over the zoom in hysterics.

"They are endangering faculty. They are forcing us to make a decision about our lives and health. They basically are putting a gun to our heads asking us to go back into the classrooms. They don't care if it will kill us and our families."

This was after the vaccines. After the boosters. My wife was back in the classroom. They'd cut all of my classes because of low enrollment school wide. Yet, somehow, for this individual, it was still day one. He had a platform. He would cash his regular checks, but he was not going to be forced to earn them in person. No way. No how.

The covid vaccine is safe. It is beyond safe. Google dangers of Pfizer covid vaccine and you'll find a litany of articles forcibly claiming that it is the safest vaccine ever produced. It was almost a therapy in and of itself. It didn't just prevent a person from getting covid. It cleansed them of the responsibility to do anything else for the public good. These people were sainted in a public ceremony. They were given a time and a jab. Every month or so after, they needed to get another injection to enhance the perfect purity of the first and second. After receiving this benediction, there were some rarely discussed side effects. Self-righteousness went through the roof in the population. Well-deserved stratification of society occurred immediately. The essential workers who had been keeping all of us alive now had another test to pass. They might not have been so essential as everyone thought. They might, in fact be thinly veiled evil delivering our groceries.

Masks are the public health equivalent of a silver bullet. Wherever they are mandated, there is an immediate accompanying drop in the spread of the virus. They are not theater (and if they are, they are good theater, just see the opening section) meant to signify allegiance with a particular brand of individual who would rather see everyone at a biker rally in the middle of the country die horribly than admit that two-year-olds might not need to sweat into a face cup every day of their lives in New York. If toddlers don't like the situation, they should speak up. They should get some political power and change the rules. Stupid five-year olds. If they don't play the game, they're never going to be allowed to breathe again. Pepper spray a guy at a dog park for not wearing a mask outside? Some people would find that kind of devotion unhinged, but it's not. It's the price we pay for knowing who believes wholeheartedly in the government. One benefit of the masks is that we also find out who do not.

Looking at the number of deaths is like a scoreboard. By this standard Florida is the worst state in the nation. It's been presented in several reputable papers as having terrible covid rules. The follow through on public health has been questioned openly. They have been pulling down (or up) America's numbers through a relentless call for freedom and personal responsibility. That's not what this country was founded upon, and Covid has finally proven what we all suspected. The founding fathers were racists. A daily accounting of deaths was pursued during the Trump era. That's because he was causing the deaths through his inept leadership. This isn't necessary during the Biden administration. They are definitely NOT causing deaths through their inept leadership. This is something that only makes sense to data scientists from Florida and mainstream journalists. Thank goodness we have them as the gatekeepers of information. We might not be able to blame the people who need to be blamed. The people who are not in power. The skeptics. The dead.

By Night

I have never tested positive for covid. I've tried. I've shoved a swab up my nose on so many occasions that it feels like it almost belongs there now. Is there such a thing as phantom swab syndrome? I have that. My friend claims he has had Covid four times. It was only diagnosed only one time, but he is certain. Four times. I love that guy.

It would be so easy to shelter in place. Stop everything. There are no drawbacks to pausing the human race. Laughter from the other room. I have three kids. They have been troopers. The entire time. I wish they were president. I bet I'd have a bigger house.

A hero is someone who stands up to the bullies in society. A superhero does it while wearing a cool costume and putting out both of his hands like this. You know what it looks like. You're just going to have to imagine that Marvel pose where the superhero puts up his hands and acts like there's this huge effort involved in calling forward some kind of green or pink energy that comes out of his or her hands.

I will strike that pose. Energy will come out of my hands. I might not save the world, but if I can change my little pocket of the world, it might build. Ultra MAGA Men might pop up on every street corner. They might hear a winey voice tearing down this great country and pop open an ice-cold Coors light and hand it to him or her. Nobody can complain about America with a silver bullet in their hands. If they can't be changed, maybe Ultra MAGA Man can help them emigrate to Canada. They will have space to roam. They can infringe upon the rights of those who are too polite to even notice it.

The inertia of a bowling ball just before it hits the pins is inspiring, inevitable. It spins into the pocket. The impediments explode in a satisfying (but temporary and non-violent) way. That is how I feel before every transformation. Maybe I could even stay Ultra MAGA this time. Live my true identity, and not let anyone take it away from me. Maybe my true life can be respected by my peers. When that day comes. I can truly live my life as Ultra MAGA Man. I have a feeling the world needs me more than it needs 72 genders, or carbon-neutral beverage companies. One more covid test, and I'll put on my cape. Go on without me. I'll catch up.

The covid vaccine works a lot like a domestic vehicle from the 70's. Sure, it works. Not always. Not now. It might cause leakage in strange places with unpredictable results. Nobody is dying because of the place we put the gas tank. That's just propaganda. We actually learned a lot by moving the gas tank out of the crumple zone. We learned about properties of gas that we would have never imagined before. It is flammable. So, blood clots are part of the response to some vaccines. Not important. We can't stop this train. Well, we can pause it a couple of weeks. Nobody wants JJ because of this pause. They're such losers. How many people bought that lottery ticket and cashed in? We don't know because of redacted data, but it's almost certainly not an amount that we need to know. That's why it's blacked out. Pfizer vaccine is as safe as talcum powder. There's a 3.9-billion-dollar lawsuit based on the hazards of talcum powder. Bad example. Astro Zeneca vaccine is a global protected entity. Ask Eric Clapton how his near death "anti-vaccine diatribe" landed in Rolling Stone. The MAGAzine who lauded him as a god for years turned on him like he was a member of Good Charlotte. The worst member of Good Charlotte. We all know who that was. A rock legend nearly dies, and Rolling Stone calls him an idiot for speaking up? It just feels like information on Covid really tested a system that did not pass. Information became a hysterical freestyle that sounded good in places but fell apart at the bridge. And finally, don't call something a vaccine that needs to be injected into my body on a lunar cycle. It just insults my polio vaccine, smallpox vaccine and even my dreaded tetanus shot that lets me spend a decade skipping through rusty barbed wire before it catches up with me.

Masks work. If this is the case, wear one and shut up. You don't need me to wear a mask if they work. You are safe because masks make you safe. If I need to wear a mask to stop the spread of Covid to a masked individual, then masks don't work. A study published at the NIH in 2021 concluded that a mask mandate did not lower mortality, hospitalization, ICU rates or ventilator usage in any meaningful way. Eleven states never issued a mask mandate. They are all over the map. So are the results. There is a placebo effect that makes people feel like they're being taken care of even when they are not. It keeps them calm. It makes them docile, easier to manage. This is not the America that questions every element of the public square. The one that tests thoughts openly, without prejudice. That's what we constantly proclaim to be the goal. Then Covid hits and we cover our mouths.

The UN reports that 25,000 people die daily from starvation. Covid, at its worst reached around 19,000. So, feeding people could be just as important as guarding the gates against a contact-traced Covid vaccine agnostic who thinks that since he had the disease he's protected. I mean, he is, but what does he know about that?

The Florida data scientist is now running for Congress as a Democrat. If a Republican candidate for office started claiming that his opponent manipulated data on - let's say- a laptop, the security state would line up calling it misinformation and sedition. Let's clarify: Florida is 32nd in mortality rates adjusted for the age of the population. This means that doing everything he could to preserve the freedom of your people and society, Desantis cost citizens less than the lockdowns in 31 other states.

This sounds like an epic poem where the hero gets carried out on the shoulders of a grateful populace. It sounds like Rudy. Perseverance leads to triumph. Why is it that most of the headlines question the governor's basic humanity? He just pulled off one of the greatest strategic battle maneuvers based on a constantly shifting enemy- it is an unmitigated victory. He must be destroyed. When did America start wishing death upon ideological enemies? Aren't liberals supposed to be compassionate? They give addicts safe spaces to inject deadly drugs into their bloodstreams, then drugs to resuscitate them back into the world for a second chance to chase that high. Clean needles are a right. Take off the mask and they will wish death upon you in an instant. Claim to have an exemption to the vaccine and they think you deserve consequences. Heroin- no consequences. Skip a Pfizer booster and you can die, and they will pull the plug on the ventilator to give it to someone more worthy. There's a meth head in the lobby flashing his taint to everyone who passes by, I think he deserves every possible kindness the society can afford. Now he's masturbating. Should I look away? Or is that rude? Compassion is just so complicated when it doesn't involve a republican.

That's just mean. That's being a bully. Be careful how often you kick sand in the face of Ultra MAGA Man. I have a very particular set of skills acquired over a long career. Skills that make me a nightmare for people like you. It doesn't matter if I'm a cop or a pastry chef. If there are enough of us, we will make a difference. And don't even ask for gluten free madeleines until the streets are safe and clean. Our way of life. It's just as important as yours. It is on the rise. I never mentioned it before, but I think Ultra MAGA Men can fly. We just need to do our chores first, work a full day at our jobs and then, save the world.

CHAPTER 21: JANUARY 6TH

Day

I'm three weeks into this experiment. I've learned a lot about myself. I have para-anger issues. Clinically, this means I have issues with people who have anger issues. They make me - angry. Crap. I didn't see that one coming. Neither did anyone else. It's put us in a stew. Nobody wants to back down. They would rather spout absurdity in an echo chamber rather than admit a single stitch in their plans might have been misplaced. Perfection is faultless. This is a very provocative road to power for a modern politician. The only thing that matters=is the unrelenting insistence that everything is going your way, always. That's all it takes to be president in this age.

Only someone vainer and vapider will be able to take the power away from you. Who could possibly be senile enough to exude self-confidence in a complete vacuum of thought?

January 6th

"Thank God we have a president we can respect again." I don't even remember who said it. It was said so often that it still bounces off the wall on a loop seventeen months after the election. It feels like a horror movie where something terrible has happened in a place and it is cursed so badly that it reaches out through time to infect everyone associated with the ugly incantation. It's not just the staffroom either. It feels like this echo has contaminated the entire country.

We can't escape the bait and switch - the unspoken pact that if we just voted for the old man the four-year tantrum from the left would be over. Nobody can believe that the result of the election could be what anybody wanted. So, everyone wants to set the clock back to an enemy they can engage with endless reserves of vitriol. I know, I thought peak vitriol was over. You can't attack Joe. He's just too pathetic. Reanimate the devil. Not Pelosi, although I understand the confusion. Trump can save democracy again.

I have to hand it to the average Californian. They don't talk much about January 6th. It just didn't make the top ten concerns of the day after a disastrous withdrawal from Afghanistan and another proxy war against the fascist funhouse mirror of murderous clowns. We did have grief counselors provided to us and the students. They sat in the cafe on their phones. Why would anyone grieve over January 6th? Was it for the kids of the people who were arrested? It would be pretty disturbing to see Dad and Mom hauled away into federal limbo.

Update: I've done a quick search of my email, and that was not the purpose. It was an effort to "heal the deep wound" exposed by the seditious rioters. That actually sounds angrier than grieving, but I guess counselors that deal with human feelings can handle more than one emotion. I think this whole thing can be solved with by the media who are asking the right questions. What did he know about the plan that he organized and set into action? When did he engage in direct communication with the leaders of the protest? And finally, why is this man still not in jail. They've been asking this since the day he colluded with Russia to invade Ukraine through a traitorous phone call he made while pee on a Chinese hooker from Wuhan causing the first known case of covid-20 (an even more deadly strain of the disease that was so deadly that it only truly could live in the urinary tract of Donald Trump). She immediately downgraded it to covid-19, a disease that the Chinese government assured us along with the WHO that did not transfer from person to person, thus saving the world. Down with Trump. Long live the revolution! Let's move this panel into prime time.

January 6th is worse than Pearl Harbor. It is worse than 9/11. Black Friday (and I don't mean the shopping day) and the Burning of Washington were cake walks compared to the day the stupidest people in the world assembled, then walked around the Capitol brandishing their ridiculous claims that the election was not valid. What kind of moron would say something like that? The electoral system is sacrosanct. It is without visible surface imperfection, and at its core it is even more exquisite. The mouth-breathing mob that descended chanting violent slogans and incendiary rhetoric represent the worst of the American ethos. They are gross aberrations beneath our contempt, but we would still like to talk about them as much as possible. Public humiliation is the only way to heal. We will heal 24/7 until everyone knows how healthy this terrible country really is when power is given to anyone other than them. If only it can be browbeaten into the thick skulls of the independent and right-leaning voters. Then it will have served its purpose.

January 6th was insatiably violent. Even by mob standards. The French revolution was less effective in getting the streets to run red in blood. Did you see the security guard who slipped in her own blood in the halls of the capitol? Robespierre oversaw the deaths of northward of 40,000 in what has been called the bloodiest revolution in French history. Was it enough to cause people to slip on blood in the Capitol? We will never know, but I'd argue moral equivalency at least. No, I'll go further. It's just my right brain visualizing the terror of that many unarmed Trump voters demanding, no ultra-demanding the overthrow of a duly elected leader. Did democratic groups call for the same thing on his inauguration day? No, they patiently waited. They built a narrative built upon truth and a series of good-faith efforts by elected officials to remove him for phone calls, being a Russian asset, and using violent mobs to project their ideas into the American marketplace of ideas. This was thoughtful violence that served a purpose. It got the country to elect someone else based on a series of a carefully constructed series lies. I can't see how this might generate anger on the other side. Unless they were just poor losers with no redress for perceived grievances presented by their political leaders. But who would do that? Trump. That's right.

Trump did it.

We must touch upon the topic of death at this point. I don't want to minimize it. But anyone who died in that crowd deserved it. The Capitol officers died in such numbers that one cannot question their use of deadly force. The country has a long-respected history of firing into unarmed crowds. Sometimes, it's the only way to get across the message in an immediate and deadly fashion. Kent State was a justified shooting of nine unarmed students. The trigger isn't just a design element. It's meant to be pulled. The lives in front of the barrel are trespassers, and that should be reflected in the outcome of their interaction. Ask the guard who shot the protester who so richly earned that bullet to the neck. There is often no other course when confronted with people who are in the wrong place, who shouldn't be there, who MIGHT represent a danger in the near-term or the abstract. You have to show them who has the power. The Boston massacre led to a revolution. Shooting into a crowd of citizens is actually the new blueprint for Making America Great Again. Don't forget that when you find out that it was the only casualty of the day.

Night

I did not think the election was stolen. I do believe that the goodwill afforded to Biden by the powerful has turned into toxic results. People don't believe the messengers of society when they are relentlessly behind all the ideas of one party. Good or bad. Anderson Cooper talked about how Trump could take a dump on his desk and his side would defend it. It was one of his better observations about politics being very close to the bowels of American discourse. At least, it's not the public guardians who fell in line. Let's say Biden took a crap on the entire country - diarrhea from one too many ice-cream cones on a lactose-intolerant system. The Press. THE PRESS would call it a shit storm that was about to let up any day, unleashing the greatest future of national prosperity the globe had ever seen. There would be no weather coverage for months. They would produce a prime-time lineup of all the worst things that happened a couple of years ago. Nobody would care about now. Now was embarrassing for the wrong people.

They don't give a shit about that climate change. They are such losers.

And since this is my last transition. I will finally show the world my real face, my real identity. What I look like right after my transition:

I'm such a badass in my Kepi. I just crave the rush. Those are the Capitol steps by the way. Yes, that Capitol.

January 6th was a worthy story. It was probed, poked, and squeezed for all the left-leaning juice it could produce. It fails to answer some of the questions that conservatives have, but I'm sure liberals want answers about whether Trump grunted or laughed when he was told about the event. It's a big difference. We know. We've been told for almost two years that this distinction is as fresh as the day it happened. Did Bubba smoke a cigar after getting his knob shined in the oval by an intern? Did he put the ashtray on her head? After all, that would change things, too. We can all imagine terrible details that our enemies might have engaged in. The conditional is sinisterly liberating. Did Trump perform human sacrifice in order to change the election results? Was it under a blood moon? Did Adam Schiff engage in animal husbandry without the objective goal of producing offspring? Why exactly has he recently sworn off eating lamb? Each side would like to believe their fantasy villain. Objectively, each person must be judged by what you know, and not what you think you know. I know that Pearl Harbor killed thousands of Americans and dragged the world closer to ideological annihilation. I am certain that September 11th was a disgusting attack on the citizenry of this country. Is there an element of that in Jan. 6th? How many civilians went home in body bags? Well, one. It felt more like the assassination of Kennedy. It's awful. It's terribly sad. It's going to be the fodder for conspiracy theories ad astra infinitum. The grassy knoll will be in the lexicon of this country, but it isn't the ambush of the entire system. It was no threat to the population. It isn't any of the things that either side wants it to be. It's just ugly.

Math has gotten very complicated in the political realm. Nobody seems to be able to count to 100K drug overdoses last year. That's not something that anyone could control. It's like the border the drugs flow over. It has no answer. There were plenty of people who received injuries on that day. That shouldn't be downplayed. It is a black eye. But almost everyone has received a black eye in their lives. It's not fun. It is painful. It's also something most everyone can recover from. Can we come together to say that violence in the furtherance of political ideals should never be explained away? Yes? Can we circle back to the riots of 2020? Can we see the same attention placed on those deaths? Forbes claims that 19 died in two weeks during BLM riots. That's- let me do the math - nineteen times as many people who died at the capitol that day. It was over 14 days, so really the riots were only 1.35 times as deadly. Granted. There was also about nine thousand percent more arson in those local insurrections. How many of the people lecturing us from the podium felt that political violence that energized their political base was equally reprehensible? It wasn't? Why? Why can't we just treat the death of people at riots as a human tragedy and get angry. Angry at every incident. Until that happens, the world will be in a cycle of explaining how death matters when it matters and doesn't when it doesn't. I don't know how they got the population to believe this cycle, but it's the one we are in. Now, back to the deaths of multiple security guards on Jan. 6th, it's a number we can agree on. Zero. The day in question produced one death that can be directly attributed to the action of someone at the capitol. That was an air-force veteran who has been smeared in the media like anyone who holds the wrong views on the social fabric of America is greeted. She somehow was part of a justified shooting at the capitol.

Police officers should never shoot without a target. If they have a target that has no weapon, they should be investigated. I don't want to sound liberal here, but I am on board. The entire shooting should not be swept under the rug if it doesn't serve the political objectives of the people in power. It disgusts me that people are still fighting for the dignity of somebody killed by an officer of the law in a non-lethal engagement. If the guard thought his life was in danger, and he purposefully aimed at this woman, he is mentally ill. He should not be given the benefit of the doubt unless that is on the table for every police shooting in the country. If we are going to back the badge in that way, it is a blanket over their actions. I thought that was bad? That's what the modern liberal has beaten into me and set me on fire to prove. How can he or she then turn on a person who dies that way but doesn't think like them. How can ideological differences merit a complete shift in the priorities of life and death? I will stick my big boot into the backside of anyone who spouts this bullshit. Lives of kids in Chicago should be treated like celebrities. These kids should get the message that they are overvalued in our society. Anything happens to them, and the greater world loses something it can never replace. We will all dedicate our attention, but more importantly our lives to the endangered. Once their problems are solved, we can have another committee meet for the purpose of taking a well-earned victory lap.

EPILOGUE

I debated whether to include this in the book. It is demonstrably silly, but so are most of the people who hold power in the country today. There might be insight in the ludicrous.

The political universe has come down to a single question. The layers of proud gravitas and mature rhetoric hides a very simple choice. It also draws a line between two worlds that is just as intractable as the population on either side.

Marvel or DC?

I am not going to label one party. It doesn't matter. Each person can choose.

It's all about how people immediately stand behind one banner. They find everything on their side to be good and pure. Everything on the other side is stupid and deformed.

My side has Batman and Superman. Pretty cool line up. Lots of movies between them. Lots of gruff, raspy expressions of tortured solitude. DC rules. How could they be wrong? This is also the label that introduced Arm falls off Boy. He beats people up by removing his arms and beating them with the severed appendages. Dogwelder? Don't mention him. Skim over all the ridiculous details. DC is the best. It's easy to pick apart Marvel. Those retreads from fantasy land. Nothing about them is original or smart. Gin Genie? A hero that must get drunk to use their powers? Sounds about right. You'd have to be drunk to be part of the MCU.

Each group lines up behind the mockery of the other. Who wants to go through a complicated series of judgements in order to assess individual members? Just paint the entire group out of the frame and move on. Better yet, chuck them in the ocean and hope that they can't swim. Most idiots can't swim. Common knowledge. Conventional wisdom. Can I get a late check-out time? I see. Everyone checked out years ago.

DC advocates have to pretend like the Hulk is a stupid character because of the label up in the top left corner. The Hulk is awesome. "Hulk Smash" has to be one of the best taglines in the history of comics. It's descriptive. It's terse. It's what he does, it's who he is. Who knew that the Hulk would be the most perspicacious green puppet of fate since Kermit the frog?

The other side has to look at Harley Quinn and say, eh. Eh? It's Harley-Hulking Quin. She fell in a vat of chemicals and now she carries around a bat. It's my, and every independent minded masochist's, dream girl. But you have to deride the other side, so even the best they have to offer has to be ridiculed. Without mercy. Like the kind of thing Harley Quin would do to Batman in a strangely large number of scenarios.

There is no thought for the achievements of the other brand. They helped build the world too. It's not just your group. Without one side, there is no competition for ideas. Having no or little respect for the best of the other side is a disservice to the process.

We repress the things we do not understand. We used to just seek their removal. Now we want them eliminated. We are trying to destroy an entire universe, just so ours will have more space. That makes no sense.

It is time to stop asking permission to speak. It's time to find our voices. And some of them are going to be lame. Not everyone on the other side of the divide has to be immediately labeled. It's hard to resist. Marvel is so much better than DC. Deadpool is so much better than Deathstroke. But Quicksilver can't keep up with the Flash. Hawkeye and Green Arrow are equally lame. Samesies with the battle van and the invisible jet. There's so much to love and hate inside each tent.

Heroes are not there to divide. That goes more for superheroes.

The End

AND

The Beginning

126

AFTERWORD

Thank you for reading this arguably forgettable work written behind the walls of liberalism.

I had to sneak out the first copies through a network of safehouses and honest thought merchants. They finally got it to Montana where people still think for themselves.

It was from this base of location that it made it to the Internet. At this point, the publication was justifiably ignored.

I am grateful for every single reader. You are the real superheroes. Please let me be your sidekick when you have to take on the forces of evil that believe this country is not great.

Ultra MAGA Man will return.

You may send your thoughts and ideas for future books to:

ultramagaman@yahoo.com